Email from Heaven

by

Andra Jones

authorHOUSE

1663 LIBERTY DRIVE, SUITE 200
BLOOMINGTON, INDIANA 47403
(800) 839-8640
www.authorhouse.com

First published by AuthorHouse 07/08/04

ISBN: 1-4184-6711-1 (e)
ISBN: 1-4184-4947-4 (sc)

Library of Congress Control Number: 2004091834

Printed in the United States of America
Bloomington, Indiana

This book is printed on acid-free paper.

I Remember

I remember to thank God for her every breath
Cherishing every minute that we have left
I remember to praise God for her loving heart
Still mindful of the miracle of our start
I remember to count the days she has invested
My support and my anchor every time I was tested
I remember when I had little to show for my efforts
She still packed her bags followed to many new addresses
I remember foolish decisions when times were unpleasant
She remained at my side not least bit was she hesitant
I remember many trials of which I swore I had my fill
After every test I failed she'd say one day you will
I remember hard times punctuated with smiling faces
It was our life unfolding together in far away places
I remember our money never collected any dust
But most of all I remember how she believes so strongly in us

This book is dedicated to my wife Evette Jones, my inspiration for writing.

Shake the Dirt off your Feet
(Matthew 10:14)

In my soul I sense that I was always a disciple
But my knowledge grew cold like the touch of an ice sickle
Understanding is clearer now, for a disciple always in training
The experiences of ones life can be nourishment for sustaining
Wise enough to know what one must fight against
How one must be wise about how one's energy is spent
Persecution comes, but it is not for depression
People will stand against you, they are not for your aggression
When obstacles come, whether situations or people
One cannot grow lukewarm nor can one be fearful
Allowed the world to cheat me, thinking I had no power
Attacking my self-esteem and demanding that I cower
Holding me down like a second class citizen
Intruding on my peace while I'm minding my own business
Daring me to fight back, calling me an alien and a minority
But I'm a pilgrim and an ambassador sent here with authority
I must shake the dirt off of my feet and ignore the majority
One day every churchgoer will find out
If he marinated in pity or just stood about
True membership really has it privileges
But the cost is high and some refuse to pay it
An acquaintance can turn out to be adversary
A smiling face rushes in intending to do harm
Shake the dirt off of your feet and keep moving on
When souls are risked foolishly for the sake of desire
When consequences eat at one's soul like a raging fire
When desire rebels against common sense seeking to devour
When evil hovers over you like a watchman in a tower
When pieces to life's puzzle aren't found in your box
When loved ones seek your pain with the cunning of a fox
When strangers stand in your path ready to defeat you
Christ is still there prepared and willing to entreat you
Yes, evil will rise against us because of our stance
Shake the dirt off of your feet and don't give it a chance

A Father

The father that I choose to be
Is unlike the one who was invisible to me
The father I could not understand
Why he'd deceive me by his own hands?
I desire to be true with honor, respect
A familiar presence and stranger to neglect
A father who leads, supports and provides
Preserving myself from deception and lies
A mentor who teaches through show and tell
Knowing that without God I'm just a shell
Recognizing wisdom is effective if understood
And God sees all the motives of man's good
Anger will fail to establish any relation
Overruled by a gentle heart and kind reputation
A father who dearly loves his wife and children
Understanding responsibilities and the need to fulfill them
Knowing the way home never a man of the streets
Love is not defined by ego or sheets
Nor is life poisoned by the vices of violence
A father whose family will never suffer in silence
Using the sword of scripture to protect family from harm
Grounded to God's promises that are sure to be performed
Though I was not taught much about being a man
I'm thankful to God for all that I now understand
It's ease of becoming a dad is a truth I've learned
But to be called a father is an honor a dad must earn

Familiar Strangers

One of the toughest things I ever had to do was to submit my will unto another. Submission is a requirement of God so naturally I struggled with it. It is a constant and continual battle that many of you share with me, the same struggle of doing what we want versus what the Lord instructs us to do.

While studying the subject brotherly love, I wondered aloud, why is it that our relationship with each other often tends to be superficial. The book of James speaks of what true wisdom is and of the source of true wisdom. Can one be truly spiritually wise, and yet be unable to develop or sustain friendships and brotherly love amongst the saints? (I know there are exceptions, because there are difficult people who enter our lives) I speak of the norm, the everyday. How hard do any of us try to get along, to fellowship, to assist, to encourage, doing those things that edify one another. In the busy world we live in it is much easier to stop trying, to give up, and to become tired, to lose all zeal or desire to build any type of relationship within our congregations.

No matter what we tell ourselves, God will not accept our excuses even if others are willing to do so. No one ever told me that it would be easy or simple. But the bible does teach us that the second commandment is to love thy neighbor as thyself. God is love and so his children must love. It is central to all that we seek to do. No gift, no ministry, no excuse will hold up to scrutiny without genuine godly love for one another. Can you look at your brother or sister and say with a clear and pure heart that you love them? Do you desire the best for them? Are you willing to let the world know of the special bond that belongs to your family of God?

The word love is used so recklessly that many people will readily confess of a love that they are not willing and sometimes unfit to demonstrate. Love is an action word. I have noticed over the years that pastors do not teach from the pulpit much about basic Christian character traits; we do not hear much taught about courtesy and respect, and thus many around us grow up with their own ideas about how to behave. We preach all the heavy things, omitting the small yet crucial things. Sort of like the uncomely parts of the body spoken of in Corinthians. Why do we neglect these important lessons on such a wide scale (obviously some churches are teaching; just not enough) The result is "spoiled saints", who do what is convenient believing they are not supposed to sacrifice or have hard times. We are in the superstar and super Christian era.

Ask yourself a question. How much time do you spend reaching out and encouraging saints in your congregation where you worship? What do you really know about the saints you worship with each Sunday? Are there valid reasons why you or I can not make time for people we gather with every Sunday? And finally, is God pleased that we are becoming more and more "Familiar Strangers"? Think about it Saints of God, Jesus died for us, we are his body on this earth, and any body that has its parts separated is a deformed body. What type of body do you belong and are you willing to make a change?

A Conservative by Nature

From: DeaconJones
Subject: A Conservative by Nature

If someone labeled you a conservative would you be ashamed? In my view there is a big difference between a political conservative and a Christian conservative. Christians after all, are advised to use moderation in all things, and though we have liberty as Paul proclaims that we do, he also warned us not to use our liberty as an excuse for doing wrong. It should be common knowledge that the policies of the two main political parties are vastly different. Democrats are generally more liberal in their views while Republicans tend to be more conservative in theirs. But the conservatism that I speak of is not constructed or created by man. It is the moral conservatism embraced and promoted by the scriptures that we should strive for. No political party has a monopoly on doing the right thing. In the end we are all judged as individuals.

Both parties seek our vote and our allegiance, but neither can bring us the peace and the hope that we seek after. I find it interesting that some in our country will marvel over how I could call myself a conservative as if the term belongs to a political party or a race. The truth however is conviction instead of race should be that which distinguishes us. It should not be our skin color or any other cultural or social leaning that determines our choices or agenda. Spiritual and moral conviction should lead all of us? My soul should not forget what the bible teaches about patience, even in the face of injustice. I see that God speaks of loving those who hate and abuse. I remember how my children should be raised with an equal balance of love and discipline, and not to be treated as miniature versions of adults, or co-laborers in parenting. I realize that what is good for my family and my faith may be impossible to reconcile with what society embraces or recommends. I have to recognize that no power, political or otherwise is outside of the authority and conservative nature of JESUS.

Where are the courageous? Who is willing to stand up and be counted among the ones who accept the conservative morality Christianity demands? Consider the consequences of our choices or are we simply to worry about consequences later? How many of us ask God for direction and how many consider God divorced from politics and our political and social leanings. Can a Christian truly be liberal in his living and still please God? Could God really embrace tolerance as defined by our modern way of living? What the world needs is love, not acceptance, not embracing ways that lead to destruction. We should not be ashamed to be spiritually conservative in our living, though liberal in our capacity to love.

Are you ashamed? In the Garden of Eden Satan deceived Eve. He got her to believe she could do things better if allowed to do things her own way. He convinced her that the moderate ways of God were too intrusive, too restrictive and too burdensome. If only she were allowed to make her own choices her life would be more exciting. The problem with this ideal is that without the standard of God we would live in a world full of individual opinions, each claiming to be the best.

If I choose to be courageous I must beware because to voice an opinion against homosexuality, abortion, fornication or a whole list of things that our society has grown to tolerate, accept and embrace as a personal and private choice labels me a conservative extremist out of touch with life. You too will be called unloving as if love requires that one be permissive or accepting of everything. We have completely recreated our vocabulary to take the stigma out of words and terms so that we can all live as we please without indictment. If our children do not understand that there is a definite right and a wrong it's because adults have for years blurred the lines between truth and lies.

When did God release man from his commission given in Matthew chapter 28 to teach the whole world to observe the ways of Christ? When were we asked to tell others what they want to hear? If you are conservative in your living be thankful to God and don't be ashamed. It does not align you with any political party, it does not make you right wing and it does not make you any less compassionate, and it certainly does not make you a judge. It does not matter if you call yourself a Democrat or Republican, as long as you strive for biblically based victorious living. To be a conservative means that you can choose to be tortoise, taking life one step at a time, not pressured to speed through life barely focusing on the changing environment around you.

Accept the Fact You Are Different

"O Timothy keep that which is committed to thy trust, avoiding profane and vain babblings, and oppositions of science falsely so called. Which some professing have erred concerning the faith…"
1
Timothy 6:20-21

If you or I want to we could just about justify any opinion that we hold with a few exceptions of course. We could most likely come up with some very good reasons for why we behave in the manner that we do. With others surrounding us who have a similar disposition our belief that our way is ok will be further reinforced. The problem is that we confuse our opinions with knowledge of the truth. God is the only source of truth, so if we are not permitting God's word to be our guide, chances are we have a very clouded idea of right and wrong. Timothy was told to keep that which had been committed to his trust. God expects all Christians to be good stewards of the gospel. He expects us not to allow our opinion or how we feel or think to overrule what we know is true.

Consider the homosexual debate of our times. There are churches that have decide God did not mean it when he forbade same sex relationships. Consequently we have gay priest and preachers (I submit to you they are in name only) supported by their congregations. Heaping for themselves those that will satisfy their itching ears. I can understand why we were warned about being ashamed of the gospel? The time is now that we will be challenged with the intent to make us look foolish. I thank God that I am not worried about how I look. If I stand up for what God says is right I will be labeled negatively so I have to prepare myself. Brothers and Sisters as you probably already know, the lost need Christ and we have to be true to what we have learned, showing some backbone. We can't compromise because it helps us to fit in. Face it; Christians will never be accepted by the world so don't be deceived by appearances.

The world will love its own. Fellowship is crucial to our survival. Seek out like-minded saints that reaffirm you and I have not lost our minds. Don't let the pressure or desire to fit in cause you to feel ashamed about whom you are in Christ. One day there is going to be a lot of folks dying to be in your shoes. They would give anything to be odd like you. Accept the fact you are different.

According to what we have

In the second chapter of Corinthians it reads in the eight chapter and twelfth verse; "For if there be first a willing mind it is accepted according to that a man hath, and not according to that he hath not." Sometimes we can be very demanding, and the pressure or stress we exert becomes so unbearable that it negatively affects those around us. We have expectations, dreams and goals that we desire to see realized. Unfortunately our expectations sometimes causes conflicts internally. We push harder to meet the standards we set and when we fail or fall short, frustration, resentment and depression often follows. We discover once again that we are imperfect and somewhat flawed.

The good news however is that God does not require perfect people to do ministry. More encouraging is the fact God takes what we have and helps us use it to the best of our ability. This contrast greatly with our tendency towards constantly seeking to do what we may not be capable of when we don't achieve it we call it failure. Failure should not be decide based on our inability to do what we aren't necessarily capable of, but rather our refusal to do what God has given us full capability to do. God's focus is on our heart and if our heart is true God accepts what we are capable of doing no matter how big or small. The widow's 2 mites were acceptable because she gave all she had. The Little boy's fish and bread was more than enough in the hand of Jesus. We should not neglect our gifts and talents based on our own faulty evaluations. God did not require the widow to give 3 mites because He is a just God and neither will he ask of us what we can't do.

I wish we did not get caught in the trap of trying to give what we don't have and instead bless God by cooperating in what we do have. It would be refreshing for Christians to choose to be faithful and believe rather than be so ready to believe that we can't. Life is short and for some it ends suddenly, so be happy with whom you are and be willing to let God lead you to a joyous life. God loves you and I, what do we have to bless God with today?

African American

Why is the African man so?
Is he merely making excuses?
Or does he remain hitched to regrettable misuses
Does he still suffer from years of emotional abuses?
Will his mended heart fall victim to broken truces?
The man on the radio says he could succeed if he chooses
If this is his true destiny why wouldn't he pursue it?
Could it be he won't try because he believes he still loses?
Can he accept a nation that he wants nothing to do with?

Some say he lives in a world distanced from his past
Will the African American seek a new world I ask?
Or is he enjoined to things that aren't able to last?
Will bitterness blind leaders against their godly tasks?
Blind leading the blind haunted by hate from years past
His anchor was Christ, molding him in the master's cast
Now his heart draws to trouble that rip like shards of glass
I see the young men feeding to their fill on strife
Few mentors chastise him or purposefully direct him in life

The old men change not, firmly set in their ways
Too arrogant to accept that God have numbered their days
I see the fathers who proudly feed young boys the bread of fools
Passing on their wickedness and teaching proudly the devil's rules
Life takes no pity on the dumb that are void of knowledge
Few boys can learn of their fathers, while others don't even bother

Rise up now African American, stop eating the bread of deceit
It is the Lord whom you fight against and you face defeat
Serve your sons no more poisons for their flesh
Gird up your loins and desire to be lifted from your mess
Reject the plots and schemes that busy you early in the day
Submit your demands and give me charge of your life
Your surrender will bring wisdom like a virtuous wife

Alone In the Park

As I listened to his words of pain
about his life and his disappointments
A story told of love lost
A family broken, never to be the same
Through his wondering eyes
Searching the sky for answers
A worn expression fixed on his face
Tells me that he sees no answers to ponder
There are people all around but he can't see them
He's drowning in his sorrows but won't scream for help
Am I to be his rescue, as I reach out a hand
I look closer I can see the wife of his youth
How did he let her slip from his fingers
Bitter sweet memories are told in every wrinkle
Betrayal of hope that still linger in his heart
A few hours spent on a weather worn bench
To hear a soul lament the value of knowing
How not to forget those who give meaning
Forgiveness is the key to freedom
To what would otherwise be just a lonely life
Walls of stubbornness embrace solitary confinement
Like a day alone in the park

Bad Communications

"Be not deceived: evil communications corrupt good manners." 1 Corinthians 15:33

I remember earlier in my walk that I would anguish over a certain scripture I had heard, "be not unequally yoked together with unbelievers". It was a tough one for me and I didn't know how to handle it, so of course I went to the extreme—isolation from all non-Christians. So heavenly minded that I was no earthly good as they say. I eventually began to see the error of my way, and then 1st Corinthians 15:33 became like a beacon of light on that scripture for me. I was relieved to discover that the emphasis is on the yoke and being unequal. I later discovered it was not the company of unbelievers, but disobedient believers that were the real threat to my walk. Besides, if I tried to avoid unbelievers I would have to leave the earth to be successful. Christians are supposed to do the influencing. It found it to be tough enough making friends, living a mobile military lifestyle having to consider the effects of the character and mannerisms of those I might desire to join myself to. It is definitely good advice to be heeded all if we want spiritual stability.

Evil is not limited to the wickedness we may recognize but it also includes sinfulness, bad conduct and bad character as its traits. Communication is not just mere socializing or knowing someone, it is personal rapport. We have gone beyond the point of attraction to conformity and affinity for those we know. When this type of bond evolves we have to very careful and watchful. Communications increases and a relationship evolves or has already been established. Satan targets our Christian witness and character and there is no more effective way of reaching that target than through those we surround ourselves with. The closer we get to them the more influence they have over us. He also targets our conduct through attachment to someone or something that has no power to edify or encourage us. His hope is that when we need an answer from God the chances of hearing it are diminished greatly as we seek a godly answer to our question from sources estranged from God.

It is certainly true that God can use anyone to bring a message of comfort to us. He proved that to Peter through a dream and to Balaam with a donkey. But the real issue for us is what attracts us to the persons we desire to hang out with. Was it our personal desires that drew us to that certain someone? Are we blind to how character matters. A common refrain we hear to day is that our private life does not matter for public service. Can you imagine a Christian living sinfully in private and appearing pious in public? It happens all the time and that's why some churches are bold about ordaining gay preachers, their private life they say doesn't matter. The conduct of the people we surround ourselves with can seep in and slowly influence our Christian character and values negatively. Even though we have power to guard against corruption, our purpose to lift up the name of Christ can put us in mixed company. Where there is corrupting behavior. We must guard against unhealthy situations.

When bad character and sinful ways collide with Christian character something will have to give. Someone will be changed and the question left to answer is who will be changed. A battle for the soul of the believer will rage on even if it is invisible to us. Light can have no fellowship with darkness so one or the other has to go. A fair question is who's changing whom? Do our friends and associates inspire us and encourage us to be Christ like? Do they seek to help us fulfill our spiritual needs or encourage us to study and pray? Or do we find that it is the desires of the flesh that are being fed, leaving us empty spiritually. Bad associations really can corrupt good habits so beware, be smart and be willing to accept good counsel

Battle Plan

Whenever I run head first into situational conflicts
Conflict with people or just a bad situation
When I can't see how God expects me to gain victory
I have to take a moment and ask
God show me your will in this
There are many things I must do
If I remain truthful I would admit
It doesn't make sense to me
There are many situations I face each day
Some seem unfair or almost impossible for me
Satan takes pleasure in me acting off my emotion
Instead of seeking the spiritual direction I badly need
He doesn't want me to trust God by seeking a spiritual solution
This would cause me to grow stronger spiritually
If I grow then I might become a tougher opponent for him
Strong Christians on his case leads to his defeat
Satan wants to destroy my life and the lives of those around me.
I am encouraged not to be overcome by the bad things in life
But to overcome the bad things by doing good
Understanding that I am a sentry for Christ
On some days my post is the furthermost perimeter
Looking out for the souls of others
Looking for Satan and his schemes while he is still in the distance
On other days I find myself on the frontline doing heavy battle
Defending those who didn't have the foresight or ability to see afar
In every battle I know I can cry out to God for help
He sends angelic reinforcements to utterly blast away evil schemes
The day I accepted Jesus is the day I chose no longer to be a loser
In my fight for what is right I'm winning with Christ

Be a Man

The message I once embraced resounded loud and clear, proclaiming that strength comes from the conditioning that I put my mind and body through. It's a message that placed my destiny in my own hands. That is okay with most of us isn't it? A real man would find a way to succeed by his own hand, right? Voices whispered messages that influenced how I reacted to my circumstances and surroundings. I could make it happen. Popular culture encourages men to think with testosterone and not rely on spiritual direction. All else is weakness. I liked going to the gym and I liked being strong, but there is strength required for living victoriously in this world that I could not get at the neighborhood gym. I had to accept that my strength has to be spiritual. I have witnessed men weeping at the altar who gained strength at a level I once thought impossible to achieve?

"Bodily exercise profited little; but godliness is profitable unto all things, having promise of life that now is, and of that which is to come." 1st Timothy 4:8.

The bible charges me to be the leader of our house. It's a duty my wife happily relinquishes over to me. If done correctly it is not the easiest task to successfully complete on a continuos basis. Church in our family begins at home and requires sacrifice, submission and seeking. I sacrifice to submit my will and desires so that I can seek after what is best for my family. I trust God will take care of me. Responsibility can be scary but my strength comes from God's grace as I make honest strides to learn to be the man God wants me to be. I strive to do what is right and best in the midst of expected challenges. It is a relief to know that success for our family is not based on my strength or my present circumstances. It does not matter if I'm traveling or at home, it does not matter if I've been saved one week or one hour, I am able to be the man God wants me to be through Jesus Christ. I know God will hold me accountable even if others around me don't. I have to be a man.

If I am failing at leading my own family why should I want to export my failure and immaturity to the church. We must mature first as God uses our families as our proving ground where we demonstrate our fitness through love and living example, not by force or constraint, guilt or complaint, but love from a pure heart. While it is not always an easy job to accomplish it is not an option. God desires for us to be men of God.

Gracious Like Our Father

This morning as I was preparing to come to work, it occurred to me that some of you might have a challenging week ahead. I've got a feeling that the evil one will seek to bind us, using the knowledge we were once lost to paralyze us with guilt. The effect of this action is to make us at least appear unsympathetic and to prevent us from leading the blind out of the darkness of sin. We've fell for it before, forgetting our purpose and calling. Mumbling because we work in an unchristian or non-motivating environment. As I've said many times before, our response makes as much sense as a fireman complaining about always responding to fires. Of course prevention and education could reduce the dispatches, but it cannot remove one simple fact. Firemen are intended to respond to fires. Christians likewise should expect to be placed with unbelievers and carnal minds, working in less than optimal environments. If we do not get this sort of assignment we should be grateful, if we do we should be prepared. We have proven ourselves able to lose sight of the fact our light must shine in darkness. Attitude affects our level of gratitude.

The devil wants us to believe we are not supposed to have difficulty. If we do, it is thought first to be a consequence of sin or some short fall. What if you are fantastic at your witness and calling? Shouldn't we be expecting to be sent to the more difficult assignments? and challenges? Don't we expect promotion on our earthly jobs? How many us would complain about a more challenging promotion on our jobs because we have proven ourselves. We expect it don't we? Still we get an inflated ego and think we should not be the one to have trials. It's supposed to be somebody else. Everyone who desire to live as God has call him to will have problems and sufferings. Our trials come to help strengthen us. We are all under grace and because of Jesus even the unjust can expect to receive grace. When we were out in the world and unrepentant, God extended grace to us and we did not pay for every dumb decision that we made. Let us extend the same grace to our enemies and adversaries clothed in wisdom and love. If we are to be like Christ we have to have love and patience with some very difficult people. Think of the times when we were not likeable or lovable, didn't we expected grace.

God does not zap our enemies like we often want Him to, instead he uses us as a means to reach out to them. It is not easy task but remember we will be judge by the same measure we judge others. If we are not merciful to others, then we should expect to receive likewise from God. When we continue to reach out and be merciful and gracious to those who are contrary to us—God is pleased. It is by these actions we show our relation to Jesus Christ. I believe God is moved to see his children love even those who have rejected love. Still as I've stated, this week some of us are going to forget these important principles of love, grace and mercy, allowing provocation to succeed. Satan seeks to weaken or destroy your witness as and identity as a caring child of God where you work and live. "God is not willing that any should perish, but that all should come to repentance" When you come face to face with those who seem to be disagreeable, stubborn or whatever, be gracious like our Father in heaven. "That ye may be the children of your Father which is in heaven: for he makes his sun to rise on the evil and the good, and sends rain on the just and on the unjust" Matthew 5:45

Attitude Check

I read a quote from an unknown source yesterday that is still stirring in my spirit. It stated that "Things turn out best for people who make the best of the way things turn out" I pondered this for a while and it makes so much sense that it is not surprising that many of us overlook such a simple word of wisdom. Attitude has a lot to do with how our life takes course. It's not a question of whether or not one is a realist or pragmatist, but whether one is able and willing to withdraw from the tendency to recite "why me" when challenges and complications arise. I acknowledge that each of us have varying levels of tolerance and patience in times of distress or stress, but each of us also has a measure of faith that we can choose to operate from within its boundaries. God never asked us to do what we are not capable of, so fretting over what we can or cannot do is a miserable excuse not to grow in Christ.

Far too many of us complain and gripe as if we are exempt from what Jesus said about troubles, persecution and living in this world. We use it as a crutch to blame God and others for our obvious lack of spiritual growth and wisdom. There are two thoughts I have about this attitude an one is that if we don't keep ourselves in check, and seek after a faithful and faith-focus attitude, we will eventually self-destruct. Proverbs 11:29 states: "He that troubleth his own house shall inherit the wind:...." and Proverbs 15:16: "Better is little with the fear of the LORD than great treasure and trouble therewith." In other words our bad attitudes is the source of how we ill-treat those whom we also claim to love and adore.

Some of you may not be satisfied with how your dreams are turning out, maybe it seem closer to a nightmare than what we imagined life would be like. Let me assure you that the answer and the solutions are not necessarily a change of venue as many of us seek after in times of distress. Separating ourselves from present company hoping to produce the desired results that have escaped our grasp. When our new plan fails too we wonder how is this possible. It is possible because friction and adversity are used by

God to shape you and I into what he desires us to be. Running from God will not produce growth but only more pain and discomfort. A constant complaint or questioning of God as to why, as if you or I are exempt from sadness or sorrow is futile. We must face our life head on and choose to have a faithful attitude whereby our walk in Christ is enhanced by our choices as we walk in this world full of negative spirits and influences. We cannot be hindered by an ungrateful or immature response to conflicts.

So the next time you feel a "woe is me" coming on, try handling it differently than what is customary for you to do. Think of Christ trip in the boat with the disciples and ask yourself what is more productive; to be at peace so much so that one can sleep in the midst of a storm, or to panic or react as if one has little or no hope.

God bless you all

Can You Hear Him

I like to recall the story of Samuel and how when God was calling him he did not recognize God's voice. At some point Eli figured out what was going on and told him to say, "here I am Lord" the next time he heard the voice. It still good advice today when we here God calling us. It is a challenge to him who does not recognize God's voice and thus continue believing that God is not speaking to them when he is. Their problem is that they don't know what God's voice sounds like. Sadly this is not a rare problem in congregations today. Congregations full of people who can't speak the language of love for themselves and need a translator.

The scriptures state that the earth and creations of God testify of who he is. There is a constant conversation going on but is often one sided with God doing all the talking and the listening. We try to figure out how God will communicate with us but our human understanding and perception of communication skew it. Busy trying to figure out how it should be; that we don't take time to stop and consider what is taking place around us. God speaks to us in many ways. Many Christian are heavily depended on interpreter who can explain and translate for them.

I've lived all over the world and I have seen many people who refused to learn the languages and customs of the country they were living in. Some out of fear and anxiety, and others were simply apathetic. They did not care enough to do anything about their lack of language skills. They severely limited what they could do because they could not communicate. They learned a few words, just enough to get buy but not enough for real communication. People were talking all around them but they did not hear them. It is understandable how they were very negative and unhappy with their lives. They had nothing good to say and did not have joy. Find someone in the church who is a chronic complainer and you will find someone who does not speak the language of love. They are in need an interpreter to guide them to the truth because they can't recognize the voice of God for themselves.

Faith is the filter by which Christians should process our interactions. Because faith does not try to make up reasons why or why not, faith leaves room for us to recognize possibilities even if they don't make sense or defy logic. It's in my nature to try and figure everything out so I constantly remind myself that I can't have all the answers. We can never know how to solve every question that arises. But if we would take a little time to stop and observe what takes place around us we will see clearly that God uses this world like a great big megaphone. He speaks to us and assures us just who He is. The things God created speak to us and our challenge is to learn how to speak the language of love, for God is Love. Take time and read your bible, learn the voice of God.

Because that which may be known of God is manifest in them, for God hath shewd it unto them. For the invisible things of Him from the creation of the world are clearly seen, being understood by the things that are made, even His eternal power and Godhead, so that they are without excuse. Because that when they knew God, they glorified Him not as God, neither were they thankful..." Romans 1:19-20

Change

I am who I am
Blazing my own trail
Knowing I will prevail
Though presently I travail
Seeking to break out
From a well traversed trail
Contrary to those who think I'll fail
Hold my breath, no I exhale
I've seen the light so
I refuse to conform
To destructive norms
I've been reborn
I've been set free
In the middle of a storm
I'm holding tightly on
Like a fighter true to form
I'm making a stand
My soul has big plans
Though I'm not my own man
I've been born again
Delivered of skepticism
Adverse to pessimism
Filled with optimism
Freely I embrace my new realism
I am who I am

Choose Life

I woke up each day ready to break the rules
Didn't want to set examples just wanted to be cool.
I had enough money and a car to cruise the streets
Not much else I need I was ready for my week
Thought I was doing pretty good on my own
What did I need to do with Christ?
Hanging out with my friends and having fun
That was the real light of my life
I'm more than a man with a worldly heart
Yet too stubborn kept living my own way
The Holy Spirit kept seeking to set me apart.
A lie made many promises I'd live another day
One day while thoughts captivated my mind
I stepped into the crosswalk trekking toward home
Car tires screeching as terror fixed in my eyes
My vapor of a life was now all but gone
Life scrolling before me lying on a hospital gurney
I can see the heaven's door I often rejected
Voices discuss my condition am I dead or injured
I need more time, death's visit is quite unexpected
Judgment day has come I don't want to believe it
I thought I had my heart's promise to behold
Jesus offered me love but I didn't receive it
It's doesn't matter now, I've sold my soul
My name was blotted in the book of life
Like a thud I saw God expected my arrival
Realizing I wasn't fit to be the lamb's wife
No place for my name found among his disciples
Lingering thoughts recall Moses, high above the plains
Repentant, after anger caused him to strike out
Remorse not sufficient as I realize Moses got in
To heaven where the lost most certainly could not

Not A Person of Circumstance

Sometimes we escape from our situation, our lot, our oppression, not so we can gain freedom for merely freedom's sake. But so we can develop into mature saints of God. We may think that we won't have to face our past, and even seek to repress it in our conscious. But the day will come eventually when you and I have to face the music and march to the beat that the Lord plays. We will have to face our own fears and devils and purge our hearts and our minds.

Philemon was a slave who escaped his captivity and in his travels he found God and was converted. While he was gone way his former master also was changed as he accepted Jesus also. One can safely say that the Lord changed their circumstances and set the stage for them to reconcile their past. One might also ask what might Philemon's future (or that of his former master) be like if not for the agitators in their lives that pressed them towards Jesus. If their lives were absent of barriers or adversity maybe they may never have heard God's call to repentance.

Do you ever sit and think sometimes what if? What if this thing or that thing were different in your life. And when the day's dreams blow into our minds like a gentle, do we ever think of all the good things that we might have lost if even one thing had been different. God did not overlook Philemon and He has certainly not overlooked us either. Everything in your life and mine has a purpose and peace will come only when we resist fighting and seek after the purposes in our lives. Circumstances may labeled you or I one thing but our responses and reactions will determine if the label sticks or not.

God Bless You All
Deacon Andra Jones

Clean Your Plate

As a child growing up, I knew what it was like to be hungry. As I got older and our financial situation got better, I really appreciated the abundance because I never forgot the times we did not have much. It had been ten years since I felt spiritually hungry the way I did when I first arrived in Florida. I know now that God was reminding me of the years of lack, so that when he starts to pile heaps and helpings upon my plate I will not take it for granted nor tell him when or what I'm ready to eat. I've noticed with my two daughters their freedom of expressing what they don't like and what they wont eat. I am always quick to caution them that when one is hungry food that was once on the banned list is suddenly allowable. It is foolishness to tell God what we will or will not do. It is even more foolish to resist where he is leading us to go. There is a danger in having much if it is not accompanied by humbleness and thanksgiving. There is a tendency to become choosy and a tendency to feel independent of others. In short we forget where God has brought us from.

There is a truth that I will share with you. Eat as much as God gives you. If you do not eat when the land is fat, how will you survive when there is a famine? This has nothing to do with the number of "great" churches in your area, but has to do with your personal walk with Christ. He is the only one who can feed us, the only one able to give us revelation of His word. I am so thankful that I ate all I could while it was set before me. God allowed me to sustain of the spiritual fat Even though at times I was not sure if I had eaten enough. There are many good churches in my area, but God did not send me to the ones I would choose. He tested me in one that has stretched my faith and caused me to know for sure of my desire to follow Him. I am thankful for what He stored up in my family and me until the famine was over for us. As I said, there are many churches around me but God did not place me in them. I had to eat from theplate he put before me, not the one I wanted to choose to eat from. If I had not eaten when my plate was full why should I complain now when he has served me far less than I desire but obviously more than enough to sustain me. If I did not eat all then how can I complain if he removes some next time? Interesting isn't it that when we are hungry we want much to eat, indeed everything before us. But when our bellies are full and satisfied we become choosy. We tell God what we will or will not eat, what we like and do not like, when we want to eat and when we don't want to. Enjoy the meal saints and don't despise what our father chooses to feed us.

Clouds Without Water

There was a lady on the radio
Talking proudly of how in her church
There was no mixing of the races allowed
Does God have a respect of persons I ask?
Are there a black and a white Holy Spirit?
Only in the eyes of man can such absurdity exist
So I wondered when this church became hers
Who made her the owner?
Did God sell his right to the church to her?
Did he relinquish his authority to her congregation?
With comments such as hers
I could discern her soul broken and impoverished
So how could she afford to purchase a church?
A church that needs an abundance of love
Love she lacked so much of
She is not rich in wisdom or in Spirit
She is not wealthy in love for her fellow man
She has forgotten that there are neither Jews nor Greeks
Neither bond nor free, we are one in Christ without distinction
Love has no color
But she strayed from the truth to usurp authority
And has revealed that if she is full of anything
It is ignorance and not Spirit
What color was Adam, What color was Eve?
She is like a cloud without the water
Full of false hope to a thirsty world

Conversations with myself

Was this really what I'd sought to become
Is this the final chapter of my story
Was that hope that ushered me out of the gates
Need I now strain to get a glimpse of it's glory

My dreams, are they vivid as they were long ago
Do I still smile when I squint at my future
Does my faith hold the commitment to conquer it all
Is there still room in my heart to view the big picture

Oh ye of little faith, dare I courage to speak out
Has your resolve, dissolved into the sea of your times
Without uncertainty what would value your dreams
Has your sight grown worst than the blind

Conversations with myself reveal the truth of the matter
My heart can no longer lie to itself
I must find contentment in that which I am
For I can't hope to find it in anyone else

Despite Life

Despite life's disappointments let downs or sadness
My heart has decided the matter
It will be filled to the brim with gladness

Though I strive to walk upright, in faith, and truth
I know I will falter still
Yet I'm free from the sin of my youth

My heart has woven a pattern, colorful, very sweet
Using threads of friendships intertwined
Symbolic of the ones God allowed me to meet

Every road he has set me on, so dull is the beginning
But as I travel down it in faith
I find that I don't like when my journey is ending

The lesson for me, I gladly share, with you
No matter where God tells me to go
I must trust Him and go do

Ups and the downs, they cut like a knife
Yet the love Jesus has for you and I
It's an incomparable sacrifice

Don't Let the Burning Smell Scare You

"When thou passeth through the waters, I will be with thee; and through the rivers, they shall not over flow thee: when thou walkest through the fire, thou shall not be burned; neither shall a flame kindle upon thee." Isaiah 43:2

After we have fallen deep into troubles or sins, the climb out can seem long and tedious. Self-conscious and embarrassment leads us t believe every one is speaking of us when they refer to sin in their conversations. Our once private life may seem anything but private, and every time we take a step forward, we look down it seems as if we are walking in place. It's hot and the fire is like a consuming force igniting any and everything around us, even our prized possessions, things we have accumulated in our body mind and soul over time— even our thoughts. None of it is important anymore.

Will it all burn up? Maybe, maybe not depending on what materials we have built our lives with. The foundation is sure, and so we at least have that consolation. But what about all the other things we have built in our lives. All the things that are not fire proof will be burned away to enable us to build everlasting habitations. Nothing will be spared, not people, places or things. When fire burns the stench can be awful depending on what is burning. If we have some rotten things in our lives, they will be burned away to allow room for our growth. If we focus only on the smell we will all open ourselves to fear and deception. Each of us will be tried and the hay, stubble and flimsy things we produced will burn up. But don't let the smell scared you off. Realize God is doing a cleansing work, getting the stink off of us is not a pleasant thing. Next time you sense the fire working to burn away the ungodliness in your life, don't be scared by it. Understand that nothing that is precious about you in the sight of God will perish. Be encouraged!

Double Vision

You said from the start, we were perfect
I admit I was somewhat naive
So when you started to act mysteriously
I only saw what I chose to believe

The saying goes that love is blind
Fortunately I only had double vision
So I had my eyes corrected in time
To say go now, I've made my decision

Dreamer

I used to sit at my windows some days
And stare at the wide blue sky
The scattered clouds moving
The cool wind so soothing
As I watched tiny birds fly by

With nothing to stop me, dreaming so deeply
I become so lazy and still
I drift safely away
To a place I can't stay
And that's where I remain until

Until I awaken some hours later
with the wind still touching my nose
The day has grown cold
As I start to unfold
From my window where I quietly dozed

I stretch out over the floor, Walking dizzily out of the door
My dream is alas, no more

To Have and To Hold

With you time glides gently by, unnoticed
Lifting gently on the wings of our love
Powered by the joy of our time together
We stand strong together, excited by our dreams

Just as the sun awakes a new day
It was you who awake my searching heart
Ever since the dawn of our destined union
It was in that moment I was assured

As each year chases closely on the heels of the next
Shinning peace, happiness and a love so true
I feel warmed from within by love we express
Growing in intensity, fueled by my desire for you

God has been gracious to me from the start
I have been blessed with you, the wife of my soul
I am ever so thankful that God knows my heart
It was Him who gave me you to have and to hold

Happy Anniversary

Faith Hope and Love

Because we depend completely on love
Our thirst for happiness is satisfied
Love has provided for us true peace
Surrounding us like a mist from a waterfall
Our sight is clear, focused together by love
We walk together towards our dreams
Trusting love for what we can and can not see
God is love, he grants our dreams and our future

Possibilities are endless, our hearts anchored deep
Though some dreams faded, a faint glow lingers on our horizon
Waiting, anticipating, we can see the dawn of new promise

Hope has been the answer to our unspoken questions
Faith, the arms that upheld our vows made in youth
Surely Love kept two lives from the danger of misuse

Fidelity Is In

Fidelity is in, though some think it not
Failures abounding concerning death do us part
Choosing to stray, from the sweet unity of truth
A heart that betrays, is like the foolishness of youth

Fidelity is in, though some think it's out
Exposing their own frailty, clear as a roof top shout
Fidelity is in, for the faithful and loyal
Bringing the freshness of peace, while refusing to spoil

Fidelity is in, though some consider it optional
Floating free in the winds, of what is culturally popular
This faithfulness to them, is as a worn out shoe
Yet he who walks without it, is as a broken tooth

Ungraceful and ragged destined to see pain
Even if redeemed, it will never return the same
For how far can one trust, that which isn't whole
For it is surely to usher, more stress to one's soul

Don't forget where you came from

Indeed if we judge ourselves first, we would be more patient and understanding of the faults of others as we see our own weakness. Our focus should be to enlighten and not to condemn others. In all cases it should be the applied scripture that brings conviction, and not condemning judgment from us that only brings fear or possible resentment. As the parable of the speck and beam in the eye suggest, we are all imperfect and guilty of sin. Thus we cannot suppose ourselves to be better or more righteous than others. Our righteousness after all has been imputed unto us through Jesus Christ and is not the result of something we have done or accomplished. Judging between what is right or wrong in the light of the scripture is a far cry from standing in the seat of judgment as if we are guiltless. Our compassion should stem from an awareness Paul refers to when he says, "you too were once gentiles carried away in the lust of your flesh." We should never forget where we were rescued from by the mercy and grace of Jesus Christ.

Don't Be Afraid To Reap What You Sow

As I was making my morning commute to work, I was thinking and meditating on the word, when I was reminded of how Christians (me included) too often look at the term "reap what you sow" in a negative context. I think it is important that we recognize this disposition of ours to help us see the positives of reaping and sowing. The bible proverb teaches that a man is what he thinks he is. This is powerful because I have failed many times because I did not have the faith necessary to succeed. When something bad befalls someone, we attribute it to reaping from bad or unwise choices. But when something good happens we rarely use the principle of reaping and sewing to explain it. Reaping and sowing is not reserved for bad situations and occasions only but also for good ones.

It is kind of tricky to master the principal of self-denial without practicing self-hatred. Our aim is to deny self and give all glory to God while loving self and our neighbors as ourselves. Seems like a contradiction but it isn't. Changes and denials are a result of the work of the Holy Spirit and not one individual thing we do to change the way we live, interact or react to our surroundings. If I plant seeds of faith now and if I plant seeds of trust in God to lead me, if I plant seeds of hope for tomorrow and today, and realize my future depends on my present planting habits. I could profit from the knowledge and understanding of the principal of reaping and sowing.

A favorite proverbs of mine states that a lazy man will be hungry in times of famine if he does not work now to prepare for the future. Whatever it is we need, expect, desire or want from the Lord, requires that we seed now and patiently wait on our harvest. Make an appraisal of your ground and its condition, asking God what seeds you should be planting in your season. If you are obedient to His instruction, you too will reap what you sow and be glad for it. You will reap what you sow but you will not be afraid to reap. One plants, one waters, but God gives the increase.

God Is Watching Over Us

I remember something that Jesus said regarding spiritual insight. He said "my sheep hear my voice...) I like that scripture because it reminds me that we are important enough to Christ that he calls out to us to communicate with us. Some people are so busy they can not give the time of day, but not Jesus. If He were not talking to us, then there would not be opportunity for us to hear Him or do His will. He also says to us "the shepherd careth for the sheep...". This too gives me comfort because it gives me power to discern who is a true shepherd, by the way he or she looks after the spiritual interest and needs of children of God. We can all thank God that we are neither spiritually blind nor handicapped. Sometimes in the midst of challenges I would ask myself why, and God would answer, Because He knows my capabilities far more than I do. He would not let me wander into that which I can not handle.

One thing I have truly enjoyed here at Hanscom is the people, in particular those in the Gospel Service. Because of my experiences I am tremendously blessed, for I have grown a lot since I got here in 1997. God is watching over all of us, and one thing I have always used to keep me humble, is the knowledge that God holds me and every other person he calls, accountable for how we use our gift and calling to be a blessing and an example of Christlike love to the world and especially to the people of God. As you fulfill your mission for God and Uncle Sam today, remember Jesus loves you and He is watching over you and I. He sees everything and just as you and I have read accounts of in the bible, He will require an answer for the actions of man. Isn't it good to know we are not alone?

When I found out that I was relocating to FLORIDA, God was granting me my request exactly as I petitioned. I asked that I not get it unless it was His will for me, even though in my mind I sensed a desire to go to Florida. 20 miles from where my lot was located allowing me to build Evette and I a house, so I seized the opportunity Thank God!

God Is Watching Us

What if God were a God whom talked to us as He did Moses in the burning bush in Exodus. Could you imagine walking down the street and seeing a bush aglow? As you draw nearer you hear a voice call out to you. What would you do? Would you run? Would freak out or be intimidated? Would you truly be excited to find that now, God, instead of by His Spirit has decided to talk to you audibly. No longer will it be through your conscious and mind that He helps you. What if from now on every time you started to do wrong a voice would call out of the bush or the chair or the clock to warn you.

Because God is not revealed to us in ways we expect him to communicate, is not an declaration of His absence. God is here with us always and it is obvious that a great number of people live their lives everyday without thinking otherwise because he is not manifested in ways acceptable to them. Let us not let that blind boldness of the world deceive us. God is keenly aware of all that you and I do. He is aware every time evil, anger, hatred or any sin raises its ugly head in our lives.

One day there is going to be a gigantic pause then...OOOOPs! It will be too late but recognition will come to many nonbelievers that God is not dead. They will learn, that He is not a crutch for the weak minded and that he is not a myth or a fairytale. All of mankind will witness the truth that He is alive. Christians will rejoice in their vindication as wise. Every rejection made and every arrogant self-serving attitude will have to bow down before the creator and be accounted for. Sadly some will have to face an awesome and powerful God and admit to Him that they foolishly gambled away their future in true paradise. I wonder what there thoughts will be like as they stand before God and He dismisses them to Satan and his devils.

The day you and I chose to serve God is the most important date in our short lives. I thank God for every man and woman that sits still long enough to hear God over all the noise of sin surrounding them. I know we can't imagine what God has prepared for us, but how awesome it's going to be when you and I are next in line, and God smiles at us and say's well done, I've been waiting on your arrival. I have something for you. Here's a robe, a crown and here's a white stone. As you look at the stone you notice that God has given you a new identity just like He said He would. Hold on saints everything is going to be alright.

God Knows

Psalm 73:11
"And they say, how doth God know? And is there knowledge in the most high?"

What if God talked to us as He did Moses in the burning bush in Exodus 3? Could you imagine walking down the street and seeing a bush aglow, and as you draw nearer you hear a voice calling out to you. What would you do? Would you run? Would you be scared or intimidated? Would you truly be excited to find that God has decided to talk to you audibly. No longer is communication through your conscious and mind, but what if from now on every time you needed an answer or made a decision, a voice would inform you of the consequences of your decision? It could get pretty hairy if a bush, or a chair, or a clock tried to speak to you.

Because God is not revealed to us in ways we are accustomed to communicating, it is not a declaration of His absence. God is here with us always but obviously a great number of people live their lives everyday without even a fleeting thought as to who God is. Don't let that blindness of the world deceive you, God is keenly aware of all that you and I do. He is aware every time evil, anger, hatred or sin raises it's ugly head. He is there when we do the things that glorify Him also.

One day the talking will cease and the sad sound of a gigantic pause will replace it. It will be the silence before judgment. It will be too late to choose, but revelation of the choice they rejected will come to many non-believers. They will know God is not dead, and His son is not powerless. Religion is not a crutch for the weak minded, and the power of the Holy Spirit is not a myth or fairy tale. The world will witness the truth together that He is alive. Christians will welcome their vindication. Every rejection made, every arrogant self-serving attitude will have to bow down before the creator and be accounted for. Sadly there will be weeping and gnashing of the teeth as some face an awesome and powerful God and confess to

Him that they were wrong. I wonder what there thoughts will be as they stand before God with no hope! What is it that they would gladly trade for another opportunity to be saved?

The day you and I chose to serve God is the most important date in our lives. I'm thankful for every man and woman that sits still long enough to hear the voice of God over all the competitive noise of sin that surrounds us. I know we can't imagine what God has prepared for us, but how awesome it's gonna be when you and I are next in line, and God smiles at us and say's "Well done, I've been waiting on your arrival. Here I have something for you; here's a robe, and here's a white stone." As you look at the stone you notice that God has given you a new identity…just like He said He would. Hold on saints, everything is going to be all right!

Deceptions

Someone once whispered great deceptions to me
Confiding his revelations, what some say I'd never be
Despite the vision given my heart that God caused me to see

Someone once freely told me all that I needed to do
His best-laid plans were a sure way to lead me through
God had taught me to discern lies since my early youth
But I chased willingly after deceit until it became my truth

Someone once told me that I could quickly rise
Reaching my peak needing no one on my side
Though familiar with the danger of selfish pride
I embraced a belief that screamed for ignorance to abide

Then SOMEONE stood firmly challenging face to face
Demanding to know how much longer I would reject God's grace
Reminded me of a few reprobates who once themselves had a taste
Convicting me to receive life in the one who died in my place

With my heart now restored and my mind transformed
I knew I could not live a life of a man not reborn
A whisper soft voice spoke so clearly truth's demands
Assuring me of a God who created life with a plan

Hate is Only A Short Walk from the House of the Unforgiving

I was reading an email from a brother who inquired about the various topics of Christian living. As I read the email there was a point I felt I needed to address and that point is forgiveness. I learned a lot of values in church that have served me well. One of those value lesson I learned is forgiveness. The concept is not a popular one though the benefits of forgiveness are plainly evident. Failure to forgive often leads to hatred. It is difficult to give mercy to people we have no respect or love for. Should we expect mercy and forgiveness if we do not want to forgive? In the Lord's Prayer there are some powerful words on this subject that many overlook. They state, "forgive us our trespasses as we forgive those who trespass against us", in other words Lord we don't expect to be forgiven if we do not forgive others.

Trespasses is in the plural form, and indicates our doing things to others that may hurt or injure them repeatedly. Some people unfortunately will do this on purpose motivated by hate, while others will do so unintentionally. Nevertheless, regardless of the motives, the consequence is still the same. Forgiveness does not mean we necessarily forget, nor does it mean you or I do not mourn or hurt for our loss, or whatever the situation may be. Forgiveness is an act of obedience, and is not based on our feelings or desires. We do it because it is the right thing to do. We have to forgive because God knows how much our lack of forgiveness can fester like cancer in our heart, and slowly eat away at us. Every time the memory or the person comes forward, we will stir inside with negative emotions. Hate is only a short walk from the house of unforgiveness.

Hate is a real issue. How can we even think to ask for forgiveness if we are not willing to forgive? How can we expect to forgive if we hate. Forgiveness is a godly principal and is not based on the seriousness of the act. If that were so we could not be Christians, because man committed the ultimate serious act when he crucified an innocent Jesus Christ. Strength to forgive can be found when we submit our will to the will of God.

Whomever is grieved or hurt, to that person it is a big deal, but we all see things differently. There are things that are done, that we may feel it is impossible to overcome and forgive. Yet Jesus wants to impart to us that while it is impossible in our own strength, it is possible with Christ. Is the tragedy of the World Trade Center and Pentagon somehow more grievous than the death of all the slaves in our country's early history, or the attack on Pearl Harbor, or Tragedy of the Oklahoma City bombing? These events may have affected some far more than recent events. It does no good to point fingers. We just need to acknowledge that we need Jesus more than we know.

We must forgive, and because Christians know it is a commandment from the Lord for our benefit. We must acknowledge immediately that we need strength from God that will enable us to do so. Seeking to truly forgive is illusive without the help of the Holy Spirit. God understand that we have our feelings to go through, but that does not make us immune to the requirement to forgive, or excuse our stubbornness or refusal. It is God's grace that is so great as we seek to come to terms with tragedies. Jesus loves you and I so much and He understands our weakness. Of course it may difficult especially more for those who do not have a mature relationship with the Lord. But can you imagine in your mind the absurdity of thinking God would approve of you or I harboring a grudge against someone, even if there were a reason for our action? What kind of God would He be to overlook our sin?

Our thoughts and ways are not his. I am not being unsympathetic. I know that when we are closest to a tragedy we have to work out forgiveness both in their hearts and minds. Some will forgive, and others to their own detriment will refuse to forgive. God does not approve of sin from anyone. I thank God for those who are able to forgive, and pray for those who feel that they cannot. It is not a question of being ready to forgive, for we are never in our sinful flesh ready to forgive, and when we do seek to forgive it is often for selfish reasons. Lasting forgiveness comes from the Christ that lives in us. Some of us will never be ready to forgive, but if we obey God and do so, he will heal our hearts, our lives and help us to do what is right.

I Am

Why is it that you will only believe
If I show to you that which is plain
Why is it that you allow deception to befriend
When you know that your actions are vain

Look up to the sky, take in all around you
Tell me is there more necessary for your eyes
It's your stubborn heart not letting you through
So to obvious things you still remain blind

longsuffering is my patience, will I longer hear
Ignorant cries, for what you can not accept
Mountains and trees, who created all of these
Confess that I am, or keep lying to yourself

If A Man Will Not Believe

If a man will not believe
His ways can't be established
His thoughts run rampant
No matter the praise he is lavished

He fails to find his destiny
Shallow courage betrays intention
Frustrations rise, from staunchest supporters
His mind, often is filled with dissension

A generation wasted, failures embraced
He sleeps on a pillow of excuses
Reaping the wind because he hasn't sown
Sorrows fill his cart, but have no uses

A man about town, wise in his opinions
Lacking knowledge, opposed to instruction
A victim waiting for well crafted lies
He hungers for the darkness of a social abduction

Discontentment shadows a youthful fool
Sinful ways embraced like clutching hands
Squeezing out the life of an unbelieving man
Sin will surely cater to his demands

Faith and Dreams

How can a man ignore the ways of truth?
And expect comfort to come in and abide
Evil will follow to old age from youth
Step for step, always keeping in stride

Seek life instead, it's a heritage of gold
Where dust can't dull its sheen
Invest in young lives with agape love
Instill the power of faith and dreams

Dark Skinned Conservative

You don't speak for me
So how can you decide?
My passions, thoughts, dreams
That consume daily, my mind

You don't speak for me
Not with your 6:00 TV voice
I know the media made you
Raised you up on the leaven of choice

You don't speak for me
Though we do share brown skin
Common struggles and hard fights
But there the commonality ends

You don't speak for me
Brown hues, nor similar complexions
It wasn't your voice during my darkest days
God stretched his hand in my direction

You don't speak for me
I don't see you in my mind's replay
I consented no power over my rights
Nor asked you to tell me what to say

You don't speak for me
How can you demand my vote?
I stand on promises; not leaning on the state
Claims of leadership framed in quotes

You don't speak for me
Even when I held my breath
Unmoved by the turmoil of November
Refusing to believe everything I hear

Andra Jones

You don't speak for me
It's doubtful you see otherwise
Identity theft, and lies from the left
Had you hoping I'd accept your bribe

You don't speak for me
Not your party's blind agendas
Brown skinned conservative lift up your face
Let them see it clearly so will remember

Youthful Thinking

How did you imagine life would turn out to be?
Just how far were you able to see
What did you think that your life would be like?
Child of hope, did you really have foresight

Did you ever think what could have been?
Had you not been hampered by youthful sin
When days were fun and you did as you pleased
Following someone, did you believe what they believed?

Passions ran free; you've sown many wild oats
When waves came crashing, who kept you afloat?
There were many before you and plenty to come
With disappointing choices that are void of wisdom

The way of truth stared you straight in the face
You peeked; you glanced, but stayed in your place
You must get free from failures; bones fall as they may
Skeletons are calling you and they want you to pay

Don't cower, be bold it's your story and plight
Life gave you a script; it's your ending to re-write
Your battles are raging, poised to steal your strength
Be wise in how your ammunition is spent

No Longer Blind

There was a time that I could not see
Myself acknowledging the Lord of creativity
Denying my own prosperity
Because of a lack of spiritual integrity

Like a contortionist who lacks dexterity
My ways and means had no clarity
Entangled and set against my own liberty
Until the Lord granted me mercy

Scales fallen down from eyes wide shut
My heart still healing from sin's cuts
Complete recovery is my diagnosis
Though once I commanded only a bleak prognosis

I will reject the collusion
To allow the confusion
Of the Devils intrusion
Into the process of my transfusion

Where is Your Faith?

Where is your faith?
Do others tell you how to believe?
How do you think?
In what ways do you receive?
Knowledge and revelation
Of abundant supply
Where is your faith
Will you even try
To believe in something
Other than yourself

Irreconcilable Differences

Irreconcilable differences? Is that really true? Are not all things possible in Christ? Isn't it true that we choose and our choices may or may not have merit? They may or may not be justified according to the word. Doesn't free will give us a right to choose to do the impossible? Choosing to succeed does require a strong enough desire to succeed and overcome obstacles. I've accepted long ago that God intended man and woman to rule together, but the fall of man changed their relationship and permanently altered how men and women treat each other. Adam exclaimed that Eve was bone of his bones! But in our world today how many marriages are approached with genuine enthusiasm. The scripture has been twisted and used to pit man against woman, husband against wife, father against daughter. Surely it should be obvious that this is a tactic of Satan. "But I would have ye know, that the head of every man is Christ, and the head of the woman is the man, and the head of Christ is God" 1 Corinthians 11:3 When I read this verse I noticed that it said every man is under Christ but it did not say every woman is under every man. He said the head of the woman is the man, being specific by the use of "the man" and "the woman". God never intended that any man would be head of any woman. If that were true then strangers could have power over women they do not even know. It is the husband and wife relationship that is referred to in those scriptures. The wife in the marriage is protected and covered by her husband, she is not his servant, and she is a servant of Christ. Her love of Christ and love of her husband are what should motivate her to willfully be a blessing and submit willingly to his leadership and example as he submits to God.

The man must be a servant of Christ or he cannot reasonably expect that the woman would place her life in his hands. If he can not submit to God why should he expect her to submit to him? Only godly men have the ability to lead godly women as intended. Anything less is a man ripe for use by the devil to abuse his wife and family. Because men and women are equal to God, the husband was not intended to boss his wife around. She was created to compliment him and compensate for his weakness. Doesn't that give new urgency to waiting on the right mate. She has what he does not have. God gave man his position in the family because he was the first creation. Husbands can not glory in what God has chosen them to do because they did nothing to earn it.

The woman was created out of man and for him she was ordained to be a helper and influence. I've noticed from the start the power my wife has to influence me which far exceeds my influence over her. God added checks and balances to the relationship between man and wife. A wise man would listen to his wife for she has abilities that he doesn't have or ever will have. She sees things that he may not even consider. My wife helps me tremendously. We think differently and we reason differently but when we put it together it makes sense. Men and women need each other and Satan seeks to keep the battle of the sexes fully engaged so that husbands and wives will not pool resources to defeat him. A man and a wife with a united vision are a danger to him.

The husband and wife roles are the order of the creation of the earth and humanity. It has nothing to do with a man or woman's worth, nothing to do with superiority or ability. Men and women must accept their roles there cannot be two leaders. No successful institution can survive with divided leadership. A house divided against itself cannot stand. If a man or woman desires independence then they should not marry and mess up someone's life living in disobedience. God instituted the position for men as leaders and it is not an insult to the ability and intellect of women to follow their husbands. Every man has to answer and be accountable to God. Wives have a remarkable power of influence that is far greater in its power than leadership authority of men. I believe even though Adam knew what God had told him and was able to pass it on to Eve he still did not interrupt the conversation between his wife and the serpent. He should have been protecting her from her vulnerability but instead she had the greater influence to do as she pleased and eventually he was eating forbidden fruit.

Where does power really reside, in the man who holds an appointed position of limited authority, or in the woman and her incredible ability to influence many decisions, of her husband? It does not take rocket science to see how wives influence their husbands and in some cases control them. As in the case of Adam and Eve her flesh and her flesh and bones mesmerizes. Man's authority extends no further than his own family, but the woman has influence that has no such boundaries extending even beyond her family.

Esther influenced her husband the king to free the Jews from a wicked decree. Pilate's wife had a dream and influenced her husband's knowledge of who Christ is. Does anyone doubt for a moment the power of the first lady even though she has no presidential authority? A husband benefits from his wife's perception of the world and the way she looks at things can give balance to their marriage. Wives need the logical thinking ability that their husbands have. It is not a shame to be different, God made us male and female. We have different strengths and different weaknesses generally though there will always be exceptions.

The wife is admonished to respect her husband because she does have the power of influence to either help him or hurt him. It's not surprising then that scripture teaches that a wife is to be careful to respect her husband. It is something she must take great care in doing. Is there anything more troublesome to a man than disrespect from his wife. God created woman to be help and encourage her husband. Satan wants the wife to be against her husband to tear him down and discourage him. He seeks to draw a wedge between man and wife and we must know that we have limited success apart from each other.

A man needs to submit to God's authority before he can properly fulfill God's purpose in leadership. If a man does not submit to God's leadership and guidance he will not have the godly ability to succeed. God cannot entrust authority to a man who refuses to submit to His authority. That man is more likely to abuse authority, for he does not understand how it operates. Furthermore, a husband should not expect his wife to submit to his unstable ways. A wife needs to submit to her husband's leadership in Christ. God will not reward disobedience to his word. Both man and wife should seek to honor one another.

If the husband refuses to accept his responsibility in the family and remains in the background as Adam did while his wife was beguiled. He too is out of line and risk damaging his family. The husband should seek to be a proper and godly representative, placing himself and his interest last, petitioning God and leading his family. His wife will not be tempted to get in his place if she is secure in the knowledge that her spiritual and natural needs will be met and is assured of his love for her. If a man or woman is having trouble submitting, it is a warning sign of danger. Anyone not submitted to spiritual principals cannot be fully trusted. How can I say this? Because all that we need flows from Christ, and it only flows in the order that God has set up and ordained. Any one standing out of the line, out of His will is on his own.

God will not reward any man or woman who does not accept his or her calling. Being accountable to God for an entire family is not a small matter. Men and Women have a struggle with submission because we have for too long abused the true meaning. We have this idea that being accountable is status, that we have to judge our worth be being in charge. Well there is no number one in a marriage. Both submit one to another. A true leader serves. Husbands and wives are to be one flesh and whatever differences we have God has called us to reconciliation.

Is it You My Love

Where is my passion, can I find it with words
Is it my desire, or is it something I've learned
Where is my love, can I show it with gestures
Is it words I speak to bring your heart pleasure

Where is the comfort, can I give it with things
Is it in my heart, or am I skilled with heartstrings
Where is my heart, can it please give me answers
Can I yell out the truth, or am I the tap dancer

Where is my true love, is she the one I imagined
Is it God who gives her as the maker of passion
Where can I hide after she has found my heart.
Will my mind deceive me, or try keep us apart

Where is my happiness, can I describe it in phrases
Is it what we've done in a thousand places
Where are my answers, of what has life become
Is it you my love, Yes you have to be the one

It's Not My Fault

"Yet say ye, why doth not the son bear the iniquity of the father? When the son hath done that which is lawful and right, and hath kept all my statutes, and hath done them, he shall surely live. The soul that sinneth, it shall die. The son shall not bear the iniquity of the father, neither shall the father bear the iniquity of the son: the righteousness of the righteous shall be upon him, and the wickedness of the wicked shall be upon him." Ezekiel 18:19-20

So many of us have fallen for the lie that we have no choice. We say we are prisoners of our past and it is the fault of others and other things for how we are. We never seem to reach that point where we accept responsibility for our actions and choices. We never seem to reach that point where we say, "Maybe I do have a way of escape" We never reach a point of contriteness required for repentance. Instead we cheat, lie, kill, steal and destroy continuing to walk in sin with our excuses in tow. Sounds like an everyday occurrence in America doesn't it? Satan has sold a lie to millions of young people in particularly and it is evident by their rising crime rate. Through cleverly crafted schemes and much in the way he deceived Eve, he has convinced many youth that they do not need their parents or any adult for guidance. They can make better choices on their own if given the opportunity. These lies have evolved into normality for our society to the point young teenagers are given power to make adult decisions they are ill equipped to make. "Love thy neighbor as thyself" has become outdate, replaced with love thyself and forget thy neighbor he can take care of his own. Commandments of God leave no room for personal options; we ignore them to our own regret We've become a nation of "crutch lovers" and it is nearly impossible to keep up with all the isms and schisms that are said to be responsible for choices we make.

Who will stand up and be accountable. Who will show true leadership and courage, who will admit and accept responsibility for his actions? There are too many medical explanations convenient for our use poised to give us a way of escape from facing up to who we really are. All have sinned and fallen short the word of God tells me all have sinned. From as early as preschool years children are taught that nothing is their fault, others are responsible for their failings. From early they began to learn to be irresponsible. Yet the bible teaches that even a child is known by his ways. If we are so perfect then why did Christ have to die? Why did we not stop him and warn him that we are already perfect? Too many are willing to blame their sin on parents and grandparents when in truth their upbringing may have little to do with their present failures. Why do we fight and struggle to maintain mediocrity? Why do we whine and complain when we are discomforted in our journey to become better people? Why do we want to have everything handed us and not work for anything. There are obstacles to be sure but there are choices also. I could have chosen to fail like some I grew up with. In nearly every neighborhood we can point to examples of those who turned to crime shortening their lives as a result of their sin. I could have chosen to hate while growing up in a very turbulent 1960s and 1970s where I had many reasons but no excuse to hate. I could have chosen drugs or to steal like young people in my neighborhood did regretting the consequences of their choices. I could have chosen to be a father outof a quest for fleshly pleasure before I ever knew what a father was. I could have chosen to follow the crowd and live the fast life.

I could have chosen the party life and ended up permanently scarred or blinded like one of my classmate. I was not raised in the church and I could have chosen to be irresponsible. Every decade a new crop of young people prove that our youth carries with it recklessness. It's a proven fact year after year that when we are young we do a lot of foolish things. As we mature, we become wiser in our choices hopefully. Out of mercy I was spared from a lot of my foolish decisions unlike the fate of some of my friends. God kept me and separated me out even when I was not aware of the change gradually taking root in my life. If I can think of one decision I made that was right in my life it was listening to the voice of God when he called me out of sin. All those years he had mercy on me and protected me was for a purpose. That one day I would speak of his goodness and live a life that rejects death. We (Christians) are after all disciples and messengers of truth for Christ.

We do not have to remain prisoner of our past. Each of us has done something that we wish we could go back and undo. We are humbled and reminded of the grace of God working in our lives by memory of past failures and events. But our past has no power over our future unless we submit to it. Parents may argue and fight but it does not mean their children are doomed to repeat their parent's activities. God is merciful and He does not visit the iniquities of the fathers upon redeemed children. So if parents don't serve God it does not mean the children are doomed to their fate. If a father drinks his life away with alcohol it does not mean his children have to have a taste for alcohol too. When mother and father divorce it does not mean the children cannot have a lasting marriage. God honors who we are through a personal relationship with Jesus Christ, generational curses are broken and deliverance is near to those who seek it. Remember we are children of the king who live under grace and our forgiveness is complete. Jesus Christ has redeemed us from all the curses of our

Keep Running

Have there been times when you just got fed up with the effort and struggle that it takes to live right. I know I ask myself if it will ever get easier. The answer may be that it's just our lot to have something in our paths that keep us working harder than others. We have to ask God for the purpose of our struggle; still sometimes we are our own worst enemy. We are trying so hard to fit God in our lives and schedule that we just can't see that God does not change for our convenience, we must change for Him.

I've tried to bargain with God and eventually found out that the only thing I had worth offering was me, and that was not much. Hebrews 12 states that because we are surrounded completely with great examples and witnesses we must lay aside every weight and the sin that easily trips us up. Doing so will free us up to run with patience the race that God has given each of us in particular. If we stop complaining long enough to look around us we will find it is true that we have a great number of people around us who are evidence of the power, glory, and majesty of God. They do not have to be in our church. Take time to get to know and reach out to other Christians.

Maybe it is our attitude that is the weight that is holding us back. Maybe it is religion getting in the way of true faith. Those things that pop up suddenly as you are coasting along, like the Hurdles in a track meet they prevent you from running the race full speed. Hurdles are not built on a track they are placed there. Sometimes by the enemy sometimes it is our own doing. We face the danger of clipping one of those hurdles in the race of life and who knows what condition we may find ourselves in afterwards. How deep might the injury be and will we get up after the fall. No serious runner enters the track thinking they cant get over the Hurdle, and neither do we, until we stumble and fall.

It's no good just to take something out of our life. We have to cast it to the side, so that it's no longer in our way. If it is on the side we cannot see it any longer if we are focused on what is in front of us. God has set a race before each of us. Our lane assignment will determine our view and optimism to finish. Some of us cruise toward the finish line while others need more conditioning and coaching. We have to work with what we are given in life. If we look in the lanes of others instead of our own, we will become discouraged and lose our view of Christ. The enemy will use our sins and lack of commitment to frustrate us. Keep Running, the Holy Spirit will supply your power and energy, and the word of God will quench your thirst.

Know It All

Some people will get mad at Christians because they don't want to hear what we have to say. We have our labels assigned to us and our message is at odds with how they may be living, in short we can be pain. I've been labeled as "phobic" on many occasions or been told I'm not sensitive or tolerant enough because I will not agree to reclassify evil as good. It's not surprising that you or I could feel like an outsider in an environment that puts pressure on us to conform. I've been called argumentative because my ways are often the opposite from what is considered to be acceptable behavior. I can remember pondering on occasion if I were too rigid or strict in how I view things. Praise God that it was only a temporary lapse in common sense.

Jeremiah had a word of truth from God to speak to King Zedekiah of Judah, but the king would hear nothing of it, in fact he put him in prison for speaking the truth. Jeremiah had words the king was not willing to listen to. I supposed if it were today, King Zedekiah would have mandated that Jeremiah receive a little diversity training. It's sad how ordinary respectable concepts such as diversity are given a negative spin through their misuse. Stand strong Christians because God is with us. Even when it appears as if the most unpopular decisions are always the ones we find ourselves joined to we can not waiver. We may be questioned, heckled, disparaged or outright shunned because of our Bible view. Consider it a complimented when you are falsely called close-minded because you refuse to be lukewarm.

Our minds ought to be closed off from that which will hurt us. Christ went through a lot of ridicule and accusations because of us. It's our turn now. We must trust God and even when it doesn't make any sense to us we must stand firm on our faith. When I think about how I am viewed as out of touch with the times, it comforts me to know that the world can see enough difference in how I walk to take notice. There was a time when they use to refer to Jesus by the disparaging terms. Praise God that you're saved and it's certainly okay no to be ashamed to conduct ourselves as our father requires, God knows what is best.

"…Call unto me, and I will answer thee, and show thee great and mighty things, which thou knowest not." Jeremiah 33:3

Landing Privileges

I have come to an understanding that ultimately what we are able to do that would bring peace in our lives with any consistency can only rest in the power and presence of the Holy Spirit and to the degree that we allow him to work through us. Jesus gives us peace unlike any we could find on our own. Perfecting that peace requires the help of others, we do not live in a bubble. Overcoming the challenges and turbulence of friendships and acquaintances matures us if we allow it. It's short sighted to automatically suspect others of premeditation or abandonment when they hurt or disappoint us. God approved them for landing in our lives for a reason. If we know the reason we can be at peace, so ask God. He is the great watchtower in the sky and he instructs us as to whom best encourages and facilitates our growth.

An airport is an excellent example of this process; every airport has procedures established for the planes that are allowed to land or leave. Planes aren't denied landing approval out of hand, there are procedures for every situation. In a like manner we too have authority to set the standards and the requirements for landing privileges in our own lives. There will be occasions of "emergency landings" where the situation dictates that our compassion welcome in those who are truly in need of our refuge. We are well aware of the potential burden they may place on us because we are not expecting to handle their problems, yet we still grant them access to us. A well-planned airport is equipped for the risk and knows that a lack of preparation could lead to tragedy and disaster. We risk going spiritually bankrupt, if we likewise have prepared ourselves for the inevitable disruptions that will require the direction that can only come from the word of God, and the Holy Spirit established as our guide for landing approvals. God knows us as intimately as the very hairs numbered on our head. He is knowledgeable of what we are quipped to handle. If the ultimate aviation expert, Jesus Christ has inspected our "airport", we can avert the panic that overtakes us,landing in our lives while we are unprepared. Our approach is one of knowing that our "airport" is functioning smoothly and even in times of turbulence we Are able to guide others to a peace.

Let Wisdom Dwell

Spiritual wisdom must be clearly evident in our decisions if we desire to reach peaceful resolutions during conflicts. This wisdom does not fall out of the sky; it is acquired from the sum of our experiences and choices as we grow in obedience to Christ. The bible teaches that we should let the word of Christ dwell in us richly. I've come to the conclusion that since wisdom is something we choose to allow or not, if we are not rich in wisdom it is by our choice. Many will tell you they have the right of free choice, yet refuse to accept blame or take a stand regarding choices they make. God promises us that if we lack wisdom we can ask Him for it freely and it will be given to us. Honest evaluation of our lives would most surely reveal the lack of wisdom to make wise right choices. Further investigation would show this could often be attributed to contentment we feel with our mediocre spiritual existence.

Because a dwelling place is where something or someone stays or remains; Letting wisdom dwell in us is another way of saying wisdom must remain in us. The truth of the matter however is that our impatience, lack of understanding and commitment seldom allows us to focus long enough to receive any benefit from challenges and victories that we experience. Wisdom cannot dwell in us richly if we are already filled with what we want. It is going to take some house cleaning and some throwing out some junk. How many times have we kept junk in the house, because we were attached to it and refuse to see its worthlessness? It ends up taking up valuable space. We face a similar dilemma in our own Character where we hold on to bad habits bad influences, leaving no room for anything new to challenge old habits. God wants to enrich us with his word, but we have not yet moved the "junk" out in order to make room for wisdom.

May be all one requires is a little additional help and support from someone whom we are able to rely on to help us clean up. Finding the right help or the right person should be a primary goal of ours. Just as you would not trust your valuables to any moving company, neither should you trust your heart and Character to any warm body. We must exercise wisdom and ask God. "Lord who can help me clean up and make room for more of your word" holding faithful and true to the scriptures which teach us that we are to consider our own tendency for temptation when we seek to help others.

Sometimes we can overburden others because we choose our help according to our comfort zones and not according to what is wise. "If we see a brother overtaken in a fault, restore such a one in a spirit of meekness, considering thyself lest ye also be tempted". In plain language this means we can't help everybody that we want to help, and we need to seek advice from God before attempting to minister to specific needs of others. When wisdom is in abundance in us God is able to break bondage. Let us seek after those who are sent by God, anointed and able to encourage us.

When the word dwells richly in us God is able to impart his wisdom to us. When the word of God is dwelling in us richly we have power available for answers to life's challenges. Because of deceptive tactics of the enemy that uses up much of our valuable time many of us fail to develop consistent and effective bible reading and meditating habits. Beware and let not any man (or woman) think he shall stand as a powerful warrior for God, if he is not able to sit down before the feet of God and take in His word. "He who kneels before God can stand before anyone" and "If you can not stand for Jesus, you will fall for anything"

Lost Soul

Words from the mouth of the lost soul
Quick to help misery unfold
Words that will surely antagonize
In ways you won't always recognize
Watch and pray he is not out of reach
Poisonous lips concealed by his speech
A calculated and well executed incision
Carried out by skilled hands of division
His ways are to too busy to scrutinize
You won't see what he's doing with natural eyes
But in haste he leads foolish men to ruin
Greed for knowledge serves as their undoing
Distorting is the purpose of his dedication
Eyes can't distinguish him in the congregation
Is there no clue when reading God's word?
He doesn't practice anything that he's heard
Arriving consistently at his own conclusions
The weak in faith easily misled by his illusion
Will words of his mouth and meditation of his heart
Ever cease tearing the church apart

Many Years

Many years have passed us by
And I know you often wonder why
I feel the way I do
I know you often ask yourself
Why does she still feel insecure?
When you work so hard to fulfill my needs
I know you often ask yourself
Why is my self-esteem so low?
When you do so much to build me
I often wonder myself why
I make you feel this way
And I find myself with no answers to explain
Can love last a lifetime, I don't know
Can love go away, maybe so
Can love be strengthened my answer is yes
Does it take time, maybe a lifetime I don't know
Do I love you, yes I do, and can it last a lifetime, yes
Can it go away, maybe, God forbid?
Can it strengthen day by day,
Will it take a lifetime, yes it may
Many years have passed us by
And I know you often wonder why

Mentor

A mentor is the inventor of a changed life
A mentor brings splendor to a dull life
A mentor is a therapeutic and good for emotional healing
A mentor is a contender to provoke one's true feelings
A mentor is a gentler way to prepare for life's challenges
A mentor is a cylinder to help weigh life in balance
A mentor sees possibilities of things others cannot imagine

Who Are the Real Mentors and Heroes?

Where are the mentors and heroes at a time when our children need them desperately? Our children find less and less any connection to their family history and roots, replaced by superficial images of celebrities, athletes and friends that may not share our commitment to their moral purity. We are blessed if our children do not live in an environment of excessive demands for conformity to ungodly norm for acceptance. Celebrities have an increasing power to persuade and alter our children's behavior and attitude by their own behavior, even if they refuse to acknowledge it. I heard a musician say once that his music does not affect children negatively. He was adamant that it is the parents who need to be more responsible for their own children. To some extent his statement is true, but I believe him to be insincere because if parents were doing as he say they should his music sales would drop dramatically and I doubt he would support that. Preschool children know the lyrics to songs from MTV and BET but can't spell their own name or count to twenty. Adolescents can sit for hours in front of the TV but can't sit long enough to learn the fifty states that make up the United States. Adults no longer protect children from harmful images and music out of their own selfishness. They have been blinded to accept a lie that children can handle what adults can, when many adults don't handle pressure too well themselves.

This is nothing new and every adult should remember that as a child we were similar if not the same in our actions. God knows young people need guidance and so he instructed parents to teach their children how to live responsibly. I expect my two daughters to want to do things that I don't agree with and I expect them to be curious and want to fit in with the crowd. What I don't expect is that they would ever believe that I would give in to my own expectations. My challenge is to mold them into individual young ladies who think independently. A writer once noted that young girls were being brainwashed into thinking sensual and revealing fashions were equated to higher worth and self-esteem. I've often asked my teenage daughter what she sees when she looks into the mirror. Lately I would get a response like "It's off the chain dad", to which I would redirect her Christian mind to the hormones and testosterone of teenage boys and how her intended purchase might set theirs hormones raging off the chains.

Some parents are so overwhelmed that they give in to their children. Particularly enlightening to me is the selection I find each time I take my two daughters shopping. Much of what passes for children's clothes is really no more than a miniature version of adult wear. My youngest is barely into a training bra but she can buy a blouse with a plunging neckline. Corporate America is rewarded with billions of dollars for pressuring our children to grow up faster than necessary. I overheard a young teenage girl discussing her love life with her equally young girlfriend while at the checkout. She related how a cute guy she liked told her he could fulfill all her fantasies. I thought to my self how impressionable this young girl was. A manipulative or misguided person has convinced her to believe a lie. Parents must be involved in their children lives to counteract much of the junk they get off the streets. It is a full time job neutralizing the temptations our children face.

My daughters have given me a lot of insight into the mindset that I abandoned many years ago. Lots of things sound good to young people and that does not surprise me. Parental guidance gives a balance to the world our children live in. It allows them to somewhat safely navigate the treacherous waters of the real world while learning in a controlled environment. I'm sure there are times you'll ask as I have "Am I too strict?" "Am I out of touch with the real world?" Don't give in; false guilt added to the mumbo jumbo of so called authorities on raising children leaves our children defenseless from the attacks of the enemy. I have empathy for parents who are worn out but I must encourage you and warn you to hold on for the sake and the future of your children. We need God's help to be successful at a very challenging and difficult task. With God all things are possible and hopefully more of us parents will step up to be the real mentors and heroes in our children's lives.

Missing Parts

We will not reach our full stature as a church body without each other. God designed it that way and no amount of protest or reengineering by man can change it. We are dependent on one another for nourishment to flow throughout the body freely. In fact each of us has a contribution to make to the church body. Specific contributions as scripture indicate. In order to be "fitly joined" we must be in our proper place in the body, that is the church. If there were missing parts on our physical body it would be recognizable right away. If our nose were where our belly button is and our ear were where our nose should be, what stares we would get. Yet we seem not to notice the missing parts in the church body. There is barely a stare in many churches if saints are not where they should be, working in the body. It's not an option that we have we are commanded to witness and disciple. Our life is no longer our own and we must commit to do what we have been commissioned to do. Some of us are called to minister as "joints and bands" and have that ability to connect and unify the body. Others have spiritual insight to see what others cannot and some minister with ability to organize and administer church business. Fitted together each gift makes for a powerful church when working together. If a saint has no vision about his or her purpose, it will be neglected. Every day that passes is another day that the church body will lack full potential. The church will be unable to function, as it should.

When we are joined to one another in love we feed off of each other's strengths, and the whole body is supplied nourishment for growth. We have no option to warm the pew, or decide what we want to do before we act, expecting God to sanction it. Let us purpose in our hearts that we will endeavor to find where God has placed us in the body and operate from there. Every part of the body is important and needed. The eyes could not see a thing if the muscles of the eyelids decide to relax and close. We are indeed dependent on each other and in need of all of our missing parts.

Money

I promise to fulfill so many of your wishes
More than you have ever thought
If you hold on to me I'll help you satisfy
Your desire, what you really want
I can help you achieve your dreams
Reach heights you have only imagined
So many esteem me the source of inner peace
I fashion joy out of materials of sadness
I can grab hold to whatever your pleasure
Or quickly bring destruction at your request
I'm the power for a life of change
Love me or hate me, I'm irreplaceable

More Power To You

Sometimes when we share Christ with others we face obstacle after obstacle get though to them. Afterwards we may ask ourselves what is it that we might have done better when in fact those without Christ don't have the same spiritual ability as you and I to see.

Jesus has given us insight we and we are no longer blind. The day we first got a glimpse of Jesus, we began a process by which we would start to rely less on our own wisdom, and more on Christ. We learned that by committing to God's way we developed a hunger and taste for things Godly. This change is a very powerful indication of our transformation by the Holy Spirit.

As men and women who have seen God, we were unable to leave the same as we were before our encounter with Him. Consider Moses, who was and still is our brother in Christ. He met God through the burning bush. After he had visited with God, and after he had listened and even after he had brought all of his excuses to God, only to have them rejected one by one. Moses finally came to the conclusion that God is a better judge of capability, and God's vision is also keenly clear. Moses left the presence of God a different man. He had power and a hunger to face what he once feared. Who can see God and not be moved?

It is impossible to see God without first believing and accepting who God is. This is why when we witness to others, they may not see. They have a hesitation over believing what they cannot figure out or control. How many say they know God but halt short of acknowledging Christ. To know God means to know Christ because the two are one.

I meet people all the time who don't mind invoking God's name in their conversation, yet I could not get them to say Jesus if my life depended on it, they will out right refuse to confess Christ as Lord. It does not take sight to be able to say there is a God. In James we read that even the devils believe there is one God and tremble.

A relationship requires commitment, which is more than just spoken words. Its' effort, energy and commitment something we have in short supply. It's not hard to speak what we don't mean.

Our commitment to Christ and leading others to him is not based on what we say but rather what we do with our life. Those who can't see God in his full trinity will continue to live powerless lives invaded by evil. Jesus said "But, ye believe not, because ye are not of my sheep…" I thank God that we belong to Christ, and He has given us the power to see. "Blessed are the pure in heart for they shall see God." Matthew 5:8

More Snippets of Wisdom

If you say that you believe in God
And I say that I believe in God
Does that mean that we both believe in Jesus?

Does the reason why God did not call us home yesterday
have anything to do with what we are doing today?

If the blind are leading the blind
Then the ditch is going to get pretty crowded

If the blind are leading the blind
who are the ones being led by those who can see?

Friends don't let friends live drunk in sin

Never Alone

When words offer little comfort
And consoling friends are not suffice
My faith seeks to assure me
Of all I've entrusted to Christ

When my days have become a struggle
Trying to live up to what God requires
I dig deeper into my heart
To draw what only Christ can inspire

When I wish I could stop it all
And retreat to a place of solace
The voice of the savior assures me
That in Him I am completely holy

When I chase after understanding
Sustained by ways that are all my own
He gently nudges me to reassure me
At a time when I'm convinced I'm alone

Not A Failure

What higher achievement can you or I reach than the status "child of God"? To achieve this status requires courage, faith, and wisdom. It requires that a person apply him or herself to endeavor to seek after the truth. It requires study and research as well as continual educating of oneself regarding the will of God. Christianity is not composed of the feeble, the foolish or the weak of mind and heart. To the contrary he who accepts Christ is a shinning example of strength and victory. It does not take courage to let ourselves go or do what we please. How much effort does it take to be foolish? If we are foolish enough to listen to what Satan broadcast to us everyday we will be tuned into a frequency of discouragement, misery, and unhappiness. Our birthright in Christ is precious and we ought not to be so quick to give it up. If we reject the idea that we are out of step, weak and out of tune with what is real maybe we could endure longer in our Christian walk. "Examine yourselves, whether ye be in the faith; prove your own selves, know ye not your own selves, how that Jesus Christ is in you, except ye be reprobates (Failures) But I trust that ye shall know that we are not reprobates". 2 Corinthians 13:5-6. Whose report are we going to believe?

Because of Christ's victory the world is angry. It's not as much with you or I as it is with the fact that there is now light opposing the darkness. Those who align with the world are angry at what Christ has accomplished in defeating the devil. Light and darkness cannot dwell together and we're an ever-present reminder to the Devil of his fate. Our mission is both important and critical. The lives of many hang in the balance and are directly linked to how well we carry out our assignment. There is a saying I heard a long time ago that goes "If you don't stand for Jesus, you will fall for anything." How true that statement is. Life and death is in the power of the tongue. God's word states if we ask him according to his will that he will hear us. If we speak to the mountain it will be moved. But what help are we to the lost if we do not believe in the power of Christ in us. We are not a failure! No we do not fit in with the world if we are obedient to what kingdom living requires.

We do not define ourselves by the world's standard any longer. We have the power to realize our hopes and dreams. Christ can make the impossible possible. He can make our enemies our friends. Those that don't understand us He is able to give clarity to their mind. We may fail from time to time but no Christian can be rightfully labeled a failure. One day when we are standing before God wearing our crown and dressed in our white robe. As each of us reach out to receive our stone that has our name inscribed on it. All of us will see with clarity the true measures and meaning of success. It is to love God with all our hearts, minds, bodies and souls that make us the greatest success on earth.

Of The Flesh

Can you hear my voice crying clear and loud
I've redeemed you before out of the in crowd
Tried it and denied it, thought it died, then
Pride brought in new birth, deep out of earth

Sin buried once or twice, out of your life
But it haunts you, like an estranged wife
I feel no elation in this, my situation
This sinful distress, the lust of the flesh

Knowing I have called thee since creation
To be a blessing and a light in this nation
I Sit in the shadows of contemplation
Woe is me Lord in my present situation

Some things my son, impossible as they seem
Are only beginning when a man's heart is clean

Opinions

If you're seeking after my opinion
You'll miss finding the whole truth
Even though I seek to walk in the light
My paths are trekked in fallible shoes

If you're seeking after my opinion
You'll miss seeing the fullness of light
Though it's maturity I seek, of all that I eat
My diet doesn't always consist of what's right

If you're seeking after my opinion
You'll find stakes of doubt in my heart driven
And though I have trust in the Lord as I must
I'm still dying, in my quest for victorious living

If you're seeking after my opinion
Be not dismayed at what you will discover
For only Jesus Christ holds the way truth and life
And that authority can rest with no other

So if you're seeking after my opinion
It is time that I get you to see
My opinions may bring comfort to life's stings
But only the truth of Christ will set you free.

Organized Chaos

Many times I have stood in a long line to wait on someone else to do something for me? Admittedly, sometimes I could have done it for myself but I was seeking after convenience? We stand in line at restaurants, hairdressers, barbers, and other places. Some of us are dependent on others because we never learned to do for ourselves. It has become a necessity instead of a blessing. Ever since God told Adam that he would have to work hard in order to produce fruit from the land, we have been seeking to devise ways of how not work hard for what we want. We want a huge return for little or no effort. In Exodus Chapter 18 people were standing in line all day

waiting in Moses to tell them what to do. One has to wonder how many of them were capable of helping Moses, yet they waited all day without volunteering. Moses father in-law looked on as Moses sat to judge the people all day long and what he saw was inefficiency and inexperience at work so he asked Moses why people were standing around all day long waiting on him. He had noticed that Moses had help available but he did not use it. Many of us assumed we are the only ones qualified to do the job. We even get caught up in the allure and glow of power and influence. Whatever the cause the end result is people were waiting on us when they should be doing for themselves.

Imagine how you would feel in a store, which has 20 checkout counters, but only one in operation. Would you think the manager was customer focused? You'd probably ask yourself—are there not more people to do this job? Sometimes it takes a Jethro to highlight our lack of organization, the Chaos of our lives. Their wisdom, discernment and experience question how we discharge our responsibilities long before they utter a word. Beware of pride and personal feelings that can get in the way of our ability to hear. Sometimes we don't know what we think we know and it would do us good to listen to those who do know. I can recall time and again where I have forgotten what I thought I knew because I never learned it in the first place. It took some one else to tell me again to remind me.

It can be hard to take constructive criticism when we feel we are doing the right thing. We get angry and defensive, but hopefully our response can be like that of Moses. We overcome our feelings and listen and hear what the person has to say before jumping to conclusions or ignoring good counsel.

Jethro wasn't judging Moses nor was he nit-picking with his observations. Moses father-in-law had been watching him perform and it was clear from his eventual advice that he was not seeking to be critical or point out fault, but seeking to help. His aim was to mentor Moses into a more effective minister, and show him how to treat those he would lead. What good are we if we are worn out, tired, exhausted, frustrated or grumbling because we have chosen to do things backwards? Many complain about not having enough time, too busy or too tired because they manage their lives badly. If our life is mismanaged then our Christian walk will be also and the effect will be spiritual burn out. We can avoid burn out if we listen. We cannot know everything; wisdom comes with age if we seek after it. God places learned saints willing to share their experience in our lives so that we do not have to wait on life to teach us what they already know.

Our Birthright

"And Jacob sod (boiled) pottage: and Esau came from the field, and He was faint: And Esau said to Jacob, feed me I pray thee, with the same red pottage; for I am faint: therefore was his name called Edom. And Jacob said, Sell me this day thy birthright. And Esau said, Behold, I am at the point to die: and what profit shall this birthright do to me. And Jacob said, Swear to me this day; and he swear unto him; and he sold his birthright unto Jacob. Then Jacob gave Esau bread and pottage of lentils; and he did eat and drink, and rose up and went his way; thus Esau despised his birthright."

There are a lot of questions we could ask about the above verses. One could be why did Esau think so little of his birthright that he would sell it for stew. Another could be why did Jacob not give his hungry brother food for free. And even another could be why did Jacob even ask for the birthright in the first place. That is a pretty high price for a meal. Questions, Questions, Questions! But wait a minute, who are we to look at Esau and Jacob as if we are guiltless. We face the similar choices as they did everyday. Even Jesus faced similar choices, however he did so successfully. In Matthew chapter 4, Satan offered to give Jesus a kingdom and wanted him to make stones of bread after he had fasted 40 days; for what price? All he had to do according to the devil was sell out his birthright and bow down to him.

What does Satan offer you and I in exchange for our Christian birthrights? If we leave the church and our birthright behind he will give us success, money, love, sex, companionship, popularity, and fulfill any number desires that are satisfying and immediate. How many times have we left God behind for a little while, so that we can do what we think is the best course of action. How many times have we chosen the "stew" of the world over Christ in our priorities? Just like Esau once our bellies are full, once we find that right person, get that certain job or position, we expect to come back to claim our birthright, believing everything should return as before.

When that does not happen, we feel slighted, mistreated, because we are not able to walk right back into where we left, and we get angry with God and the saints. We may even go as far as to despise our sisters and brothers never even considering looking at the choices we made. Why is it that everyone else is the problem except us?

Satan continually holds out his hands, hawking his wares, trying to entice us to put our priorities and interest before what God has called us to do. Sometimes our desires are in line with the will of God and his purposes, and there is no problem. At other times his sales pitch intrigues us and we bite. When God has not agreed with our request or we do accept His guidance we sellout. We accept Satan's lies and offers and rationalize our choice. Like Esau we ask, what good is my birthright, what good is being a Christian if I'm lonely, or don't have enough money. So we shoot for the stars in this world at a price far too high to pay, and that price is our birthright and the promises that God has given us. Surely Satan will come to collect his dues if we owe him, this is after all his world system that we live in. How many Christians have quenched the Holy Spirit in order that they might achieve the fulfillment of their personal hunger?

We should each ask ourselves every now and then, what is it Lord that I have sold you out for? Satan will promise us whatever we want to hear, in order to persuade us to give up what he knows he cannot take away from us. Beware saints it may taste good for the moment, and it may even fill our belly to satisfaction, but the cost will not be free. Let us examine ourselves that we may be able to say before the Lord that we will honor and cherish our birthright, and we cannot be bought for any price.

Power of the Wind

Her entrance is made without an invite
From where she came is unknown and undetermined
Her forcefulness a surprise bringing a woeful murmur
Oblivious to souls seeking a shelter's respite
Growing stronger through the day from the calm of night
A feign anger is displayed, mother is back on parade
Who can escape, coordinating a successful evade
Her bark is only a shadow of her bite

Her record is unblemished opponents try in vain
A sort of victory is only for those who flee
Wisely abdicating to so natural a power
Recognizing that such a decision brings hope again
Refuge from a power of such magnificent display
For the lady of nature is a strong tower

Questions

Do I still think about you always
Like I did from our spontaneous start
When I speak or hear your name lately
Does that joy still stir in my heart

When I look at you do I still size you
Like I've done often from your head to toe
Has my commitment to you and our future
Been entrenched stronger than ever before

When I ask myself these sort of questions
Can I answer still quickly so
Since you can't read what's on my mind
Here's some answers I think you should know

Of all that you've come to expect of me
My actions don't always reflect my best
Still every equation concerning you plus me
Still adds up to yes my love, I answer yes

September A Nation Has Changed

A nation has changed
Never again, can it return the same
It's feign body of civility
Tested, resuscitated and transformed
Death has ushered in new life
Revealed is the long forgotten daughter
Once toppled in the wake of family ambitions
Dysfunctional, no longer Belle of the world
Yet still, even a wounded patriarch
Can not sit still against his family's assault
Ideals arise from the ashes, a sibling wrapped in pain
Sees comfort ascending tall above the horizon
Beckoning for peace and genuine civility
Knowingly satisfied, life won't be the same
Seeking that which trial by fire proclaims
A nation has changed
For the good it seeks not the past again
Hoping that, from past errors refrained
A once naive daughter can yet again
Receive her glory and mend her ways

Servant and Hireling

A servant springs to action through her heart of love
Her mind is free of concern with what others are thinking of
Motives are sincere devoid of any attached strings
She stands ready for whatever the challenges might bring
A Hireling stands silent plotting to win her demands
Her mind is overly consumed with all that she plans
Her help may be available but it will come with a price
For in any profitable endeavor she is sure to want a slice
A servant is humble, willing to stand with the team
Unity as his guide as he strives toward his dream
Focused on the vision all that he does is to glorify Christ
This servant's whole desire is to be a blessing in life
A hireling is satisfied when opportunity for him abounds
If there is profit to be had you'll surely see him around
His memory is kind of short so he forgets what he deserves
Make ready concessions now if you want to see him serve
Grace is bestowed in abundance is never to be hired out
Serving is a sure way in the kingdom to gain clout
So grow up in Christ seizing upon every opportunity
To serve one another in a spirit of loving unity

Shadow

Born into poverty, yet not lacking in spirit
My soul screamed loudly, but no one could hear it
I saw myself clearly, but we couldn't communicate
I knew I must rebuke the devourer, cast out my fate
I searched for who I was not knowing where to look
Because I was so confused, I was often misunderstood
My heart carried a burden, disguised as a smile
Poverty brought me heaviness, since I was a child
Would I shrivel up and fade, succumb to my own pity
Was I destined to be a drain or blight on my city
These thoughts were once in my head, till my heart cast them out
If I was to be a survivor, I had to dispense of my doubts
I must recognize and honor, my creator and Lord
If I continued to live defeated, what was I breathing for
Spread before me was death and life, on my destiny's table
I know now that If I'm willing, surely my God is able

Sin Is Like A Weed

I have heard before, the lament from friends that are trying to live by faith but don't know what else to do. They say they are willing to make sacrifices but they cannot see how to do it. They say they are committed, but just can't see their efforts through like they should. What they are really saying is they are failing in their faith. And what they do not understand is that struggles and trials are part of the process, and may not be a problem at all. Their struggles can be signs of the little faith that they need to feed so that it becomes greater. Blurred vision as a result of living in a society that rewards success has them confused and frustrated.

When I was a child I was reminded over and over again that hard work and honest effort were not a sign of weakness. Perseverance was encouraged and worn as a badge of honor. Sadly though, a lot has changed since I was a child and struggles can easily be perceived as failure. Athletes no longer remain with one team for a career in search of more money and coaches do not get invited back if they don't produce a champion quickly. We have moved far away from the principal of hard work perseverance and success, replaced by the self-made men or celebrities as the standard. Time and support necessary to get establish is a luxury that most do not want to pay for and prefer instant gratification and overnight sensations instead. Have our expectations gone too far are we unrealistic?

We are discarding a reasonable standard so that we can adopt a weaker one pleasing to our desires. The reversed standard of measure is destined to further erode the moral coastline of our nation? All it takes is a few generations of spoiled children who believe they have a right to be successful, that they are owed peace and prosperity; they deserve to live without struggle, disease or bad health. Producing a generations of misguided and misinformed citizens. Citizens who will introduce new laws and shape the next generation of young minds. Looking for something for free or with little effort. Not much different from past generations except in one area. Their attitude is now accepted and taught as a reasonable expectation.

Instead of evolving into a nation of slothful inhabitants we must fight back. We have to know that we must do more than just have enough faith to hang and whine. We cannot give in to politically correct views and deceptive cries from the world. Our purpose demands greater effort than satisfaction with minimal effort. We are encouraged instead to see even a minimum amount of faith as that which is necessary to start a change in our own attitude. We begin by believing in what God says we are each able to do through Christ. We start at the root of the problem, which is unacknowledged sin, which even in small amounts will eventually spread and take over. Sin is like a weed, if you do not kill it at the root it will grow back into your life.

Skeptical to Faithful

God's word is living and the word is able to get beyond what we advertise. People see every day only what we want them to see about us. Unless God grants a discerning spirit others won't know or understand what we are experiencing and neither can they know our intentions. We put up a myriad of defenses and protective barriers to protect ourselves from hurt, disappointment, and rejection. Honestly some of us are difficult to reach out to because we retreat and do not reciprocate the offers of fellowship from others. Satan loves it when we don't reach out to one another because it's easier for him to defeat the loner when there is no support.

Truth is we place limits on God, spelling out when, where and how we will cooperate with Him. Instead of following the unction of the Holy Spirit, we dictate our own rules. The result is a congregation full of skeptics and strangers. Even after years of worshipping at the same church, there are people who still do not know their fellow parishioners. I remember when I used to think I controlled God in my life. Sure God granted me his permissive will and allowed me to do as I thought was wise. At any moment he could have said "not so", I was not the one in control, I just thought I was. After spinning my wheels for a few years I eventually woke up to the truth and began the process toward surrendering my entire life. No longer holding back what I thought He could not fix, or using habits or my likes and dislikes to determine where I would go and who I would cultivate fellowship with. God changed me from skeptical to faithful.

Faithful saints trust God for what they do not understand and they follow him to places they do not know. They allow God to mend hurts and disappointments and restore and repair trust. They are more eager to submit than to resist or use excuses. God knows the thoughts and the intents of our hearts, even if we don't let on to others around us how we feel. He knows where we have been and where we are going. The façade that other saints see is not what God sees. We can hide the truth from the world, but we cannot hide our true motivations, fears and thoughts from God! We are truly "naked" before him just as Adam and Eve were placed in the garden naked. We cannot hide, nor can we disguise who we really are; God knows the truth about us. He recognizes we have challenges of our own to overcome, and still He calls us to work for Him. Lets not remain skeptical knowing that God sees all and is able cultivate faithfulness in us. Resist using excuses and trusting ourselves so that He can guide us.

Snippets of Wisdom

My job is like a cruiser
As it floats down the autobahn
In the fast lane
Towards the town of complete
Friends are like lottery tickets
Sometimes you win
Sometimes you lose
And sometimes you hit the jackpot
Pop, Pop, the weapon goes bang
Life has ended for another in a gang
Crash is the sounding of broken glass
Tragedy comes to visit those who live too fast

Solid Foundation

I wanted to build you completely
Of only the very best stones
I sort of knew from the beginning
I should not attempt this task alone

Instead I gave it my full attention
Withdrew from within, only my best
Still aware you deserved much more
And if I failed there would be much regret

So inspected you many times for cracks
Checking you over and over again
But on the day that you faced a big storm
I discovered you could not sustain

My lesson I learned the hard way
That if I choose to build you alone
I can only build a foundation of sand
Though my heart desires one made of stone

Some Things

Some things are automatic
Like some of the things you do
Some things make like terrific
Like the things I see in you
Some things are clearly destined
Like our love we have discovered
Some things feel so very wonderful
Like the moment we found each other
Some things are good things
And some things are true
I knew you were something
The moment I laid eyes on you

Dedicated to Evette

Speak and God Will Do the Work

I was asked a question once in regards to Moses not making it to the Promised Land. Of Course I'm speaking of the physical Promised Land and not the spiritual one, but the moral lesson is still important. We must be careful to continue in good works lest we forget whose we are and who we belong to, letting our faith slip. I would like to share my thoughts with you. I would also like to encourage you to stay with what God has required of you. We have good intentions towards our brothers and sisters in Christ, but ultimately it is God, whom you and I must please even when others complain or are not able to understand why we do what we do. Seek ye first the kingdom of God!

In Numbers Chapter 20 we read the story of how Moses lost his cool. Yes, the man of God called and chosen, the one who stood at the burning bush smites the rock not once but two times. I wonder how many were so busy murmuring and caught up in their needs they didn't have time to pray for their leader Moses. All he was required to do was speak. Kind of makes me think of all the mercy of God from the times I have gone beyond what God told me to do and did not suffer His displeasure. Moses did not obey God's instructions. God told him to speak to the rock in the presence of the children of Israel, and water would come forth from it.

Moses hit the rock and water still came forth from the rock and children of Israel did drank, but Moses paid a heavy price for his improvisation. Can you see the important lessons in this for us? Place yourself back in time and in Moses' shoes. The people are rebelling against you and Aaron because they have no water. Because they cannot see or understand how God is leading you, they question why you have led them to a place with no water. You are frustrated, they are frustrated and angry because in their eyes you may as well have stuck a knife in them and killed them a lot quicker. You become heavy with grief and anger because of their blindness. You think of all the other miracles God has shown you, and provided to them, yet they have quickly forgotten. So in frustration you lash out at them, forgetting that in anger you cannot do what God wants you to do, forgetting God only asked you to speak, nothing difficult, nothing else. And now you have a problem.

How many times have we let others cause us to lose our blessing? God does not need our help, nor does He require that we do anything except allow Him to reveal Himself in our lives. How many times have we let anger and frustration cause us to lash out and allowed frustration to cause us to momentarily lose our focus. Just long enough to cause some damage. Will the reactions of others, or testy situations lead us to our own solutions. Moses let the complaining and ungrateful attitude of those he was leading, cause him to lose sight of what God sent him to do. God still allowed water to come forth. Our disobedience cannot alter God's plan. God wanted water to come forth, and it did. What an eye opener when we consider, just because we get what we are searching for we are not exempt from the consequences we will certainly have to pay.

The principle of reaping and sowing stands true. It is not strange for man to think the end justifies the means. That is the attitude of our world we live in. God's children must resist this kind of thinking. We can't just concentrate or focus on reaching some goal, or silencing our critics. This can lead to cheating and dishonesty in our hour of frustration. God is reminding us through this story of the disobedience of Moses that He reigns all by Himself. We cannot alter His plans, we can not decide to add our little twist as we see fit. We can not allow Satan to tempt us through anger to disobey God. We may get what we were seeking, but the price we pay ultimately will be high, and probably too high for us to pay. It's not worth it. Imagine trying so hard to reach a goal, only to see it slip from view. Moses got a glimpse, but he never got to realize his dream. How many of us today forget this important point of God's way and do things our way. In the end we see what we want, fulfilled and evident in the lives of others. We get to see it from a good vantage point just like that mountain Moses stood on, but because we chose our way we never get to reach our Promised Land. All I can think is Lord have mercy on me that I do things the right way.

The Folly of Hate

They entered into a battle of wits
Undeterred by their lack of ammunition
And only after they reached a crossroad
Did their lack arouse any suspicion?
Encouraged by ego, fools motivation
They continued in their war of words
Explosive temperaments, and shallow defenses
Hastily built in past insincerity
So panic ensues, with neither subdued
Pleading for allies, or combatants by induction
But what they did not know, did hurt them so
For mutual hate assures mutual destruction

The Gift of Hope

Where there is hopelessness
Empty lives sprout freely
Gifts sent from God sit idle
Wasting away
Excuses, Abuses, Misuses, Elusive dreams
Chronicles of a life unlike what it seems
Remember the good old days
Were they really the bad days?
Of sorrow, poverty and brokenness
The rich who are poor with starving minds
Blind men with eyes wide open
The ditch seems to follow where they lead
Darkness on a rainy day
No sun, just clouds
Covering a warm heart, with coldness
Altering the perception of the future
Sapping the strength of whatever boldness remains
There is a need for change
To get back on the straight and narrow again
Come and gone, chasing after where they don't belong
Leaving no marks, just one large faded trail
Evidence that they did not prevail
Seduction and abduction of grand ideas
Construction and obstruction of a young one's zeal
Imprisoned by a thoughtless mind
It can't see or understand how victory resides within man
Struggles that were visited once to an oppressed people
There is shame in what is remembered
But gratefulness abounds still
History recites what was once pushed to the back shelf
Opening the book reveals a few pages are missing
Accomplishments buried deep, God will fill in the gap
The future does not have to be controlled by the past
We have been rescued by the power of love that last
Discouragement fades as rejoicing takes over through hope
No one can stay the same when in Christ his faith remains

The Hitchhikers

On a warm southern night
Something occurred not so right
As we held out our thumbs
Seeking a free ride to bum
It was I and my friend
Who opened the doors to get in
A big dark automobile
He sped away spinning wheels
We thank him nervously, being courteous
Glances at each other, we were nervous
Had this man broken some kind of law
Were those really clamped hands that we saw
Pressing the accelerator to the floor
The speed got up to 90 miles or more
Then suddenly, no warning, he just stopped
We asked no questions, leaping out

The Truth

Acknowledge and make known the truth
Declare it clearly and confess it
I am in a fallen state unable to see
There's no escape after struggling with my part
And after words of wisdom penetrate my heart
With chances of conversion after much resistance
How can doubts still remain?
God won't desert me and he won't let go
Why am I so stubborn, why can't I listen?
I'm a good person; aren't I decent?
I'm haunted by a nagging conviction
None are righteous I've read
Decent people are a dime a dozen
A man's ways are right in his own eyes
So there has to be a higher being than I
I can't be supreme over myself?
If I'm supreme why must I die?
Surely I would not allow this
Among two truths which is a lie?
Can there be more than one truth really?
One day I will see the truth as it is
One day there will be a judgment

Prayer Answered

You are in my prayers you need not ask.
I make the commitment freely accepting my task
Troubles enter our lives sometimes like storms
Invading our sanctuary at times for no reason at all

Trust in your faith to pursue prayer and study.
Surrender not to your problem seek to rise above it
I was told once of the plight of a certain man
With misfortune hard to view as a part of God's plan

This poor soul had shot himself in the head
Fortunately it was not a bullet but a dart instead
How this could happen he didn't understand
Tragedy befalling such a faithful man

Very bad things happen to very good people
Since the dawn of time has proven a very great teacher
The injured was transported for emergency care
Admitted to a hospital where he lay in despair

The dart quickly removed followed with a CAT scan
A surprise discovered which was shocking to the man
A tumor found in his brain that he never knew he had
Had been successfully removed and for this he was glad

His lesson learned clearly regarding faith during trials
God answer prayers in miraculous style

The Unknown Poets

A group of unknowns cast impassioned pleas
Shaped into words for observers to read
Hindsight is rampant, though the heart is betrayed
Expression flows freely while responses are delayed
Poetic expressions expounding upon emotions through rhyme
Speaking what the heart sees from a snapshot in time
Strangers conversing in a collage of different voices
From the treasury of our souls flow a variety of choices
Poetry in motion canvassing the breadth of one's life
Giving a soulful expression to whatever we write
From the privacy of the mind, dare we reach out to give?
That others might get a glimpse of the lives that we live
Impassioned expressions as never before heard
Written and shaped with the distinct voice of words
Strangers, unknowns share a common goal to rejoice
Through the simplicity of our words emerges a poetic voice

The Urge of My Heart

The urge of my heart beats against the wind of life
It is far stronger than even I had imagined
Expression of truth on my face aren't always suffice
For when I'm unhappy my smile is worn as a badge of gladness

The passion of my thoughts are the fire of hopes and dreams
Raging far from what present capabilities deliver
Toward a place that I've traveled often on my mind's stream
To wait patiently at the crest of hope's rising river

The peace of my faith is like a mediator skilled and strong
Debating against every sign of fear or disappointment
It's my advocate protecting me, shielding me from doubts throng
Pointing straightway toward my future's victorious anointing

The Urge of my heart beats against the wind of life
It is far more hopeful or thankful than my lips ever reveal
Beating quickly at very imagination of my possibilities for good
A hopeful heart makes so many possibilities real

They

They were diagnosed with the symptoms of Adam and Eve
Unsure of who they wanted to please
Stepping out boldly into the unknown
Yet unprepared to reap what they had sown

They moved on to a new life, another place
An Attempt to start over, adjust their taste
The apple of their eye, which once brought them shame
Yet determined still, they start over again

They were a couple still in their youth
despite their problems, they want to break through
In a world of snakes and fruit forbidden
They are learn from experience truth is not hidden

Through The Night

I walked to my car and opened the door
Quickly I hopped in, pressed the pedal to the floor
Cruising sixty miles per hour in a 35 zone
Not especially attentive as I head towards home

But a young woman sitting in a big blue car
Is clocking my speed with her police radar
I put my brakes in action, dimmed my high beam lights
Then on come her blue ones, lighting up the night

I'm thinking, what a bummer as I coast to the curb
As right behind my auto, she gracefully swerves
I expect an authoritarian, someone slightly wicked
Instead she was sort of nice, except for the ticket

She told me where to pay and noticed my license was new
I replied, I got it today, and yes my new car too
So I would suffer a loss of funds, my wallet would be light
I reaped what I'd sown for speeding through the night

Time

Taking time for granted, surely to a fault
Like chances we take with our lives
Wasting a valued friend, sure to be caught
forgetting the decades of lessons gone by

So treat time wisely, you'll need him again
He's has a reputation for no compromise
Always claiming what we fail to defend
It's through our actions that we oft despise

Running man, open ears to my counsel
Time waits for none, listen while you're able
Sorrow not at the fortunes of scoundrels

Used properly, you can move mountains
Wisdom declares, that if you live unaware
He won't wait, and your youth has no fountain

Troubled Water

"For an angel went down at a certain season into the pool, and troubled the water: whosoever then first after the troubling of the water stepped in was made whole of whatsoever disease he had. And a certain man was there, which had infirmity thirty and eight years. When Jesus saw him lying there and knew that he had been now a long time in that case, he saith unto him, Wilt thou be made whole? The impotent man answered him, Sir, I have no man, when the water is troubled, to put me into the pool: but while I am coming, another steppeth down before me. Jesus saith unto him, Rise, take up thy bed, and walk. And immediately the man was made whole, and took up his bed, and walked: and on the same day was the Sabbath."
John 5:4-9

We are living in the time of faith and are not limited by the time and seasons. An important lesson to learn is that we should not focus more on the process more than we do on the deliverer who is Christ. Past failures should not be allowed to prohibit us from receiving our blessings. Jesus already new the man's condition, he simply asked him if he wanted to be healed. His first response was to recount what he did not have not understanding that Jesus has what we lack. He focused on the process and his condition nearly pitying himself. Interestingly Jesus did not join him in his reason and excuses of why he couldn't, Jesus wanted to know if he was willing, so he asked him more directly the second time. Get up and get on with your life. I am here to deliver you and it is not dependent on what you have because you can do all things through me.

The man was there but he was not there. Jesus had already healed him. Why would Jesus tell him to do something that he was not able to do? The man was healed and then he got up and there is no indication where he asked for it. God knows what we need if we are to be able to do what he ask of us. His healing was immediate when Jesus healed him. He had mercy on him despite his lack of faith. It's like that sometimes isn't it?

We have struggled for a time, maybe years with a problem, condition, a hope and we don't expect a miracle because it hadn't happen so far. Yet we still go through the motions just like the man did returning to the pool time after time not expecting any opportunity, not faithful, not sincere, just wishing and going though the process. We hang out at the Alter and we pray over and over again. We fast and we do everything but believe. God is seeking to help us but we are to busy looking for a handout from man.

The man didn't even remember that light and darkness can't dwell together and thus Jesus presence at the pool was enough to send his sickness packing. Truth of the matter is that God wants to bring us through our infirmities that we might trust in him and not the process.

Two Sides to The Story

Email has allowed us to send spiritual stories and sometimes what passes for spiritual stories around the globe. I've heard some good ones and some inspiring ones. Every now and then I hear a really bad one that causes me to question what the author was thinking when he wrote it. One such story floating around is the one about the men bursting into the church and all members who flee are suppose to be hypocrites. This view is simplistic and misleading in its attempt to describe faithfulness.

Where in the bible does it require us or even asks of us to test one another? Why would a Christian even participate in such an activity to scare their sisters and brothers? Human emotion is the great variable in our walk in Christ. Our reaction to fear is not basis for judging our character alone. We must consider the whole person and their Christian walk, not one isolated incident. God is not a one mistake God so we should not confuse him with the way we would think or reason. If the people who fled the church after a threat were hypocrites because they fled then what should we think of Peter who denied Christ not once but twice out of fear of what would happen to him if he identified himself as a follower of Christ to those questioning him?

I believe the story to be an unfair characterization. Paul warned us not to judge after the outward appearance. The fact that some remained and did not flee, are they to be viewed as more righteous by their single act? What if stayed because they panicked and froze, or what if they run the next time? Will they somehow lose that righteousness? Righteousness is not something we can earn by reacting or behaving in a certain manner. Righteousness is through Christ! Beware not to get caught up in religious sounding things. Was it the fear of dying (a human emotion to a perceived threat) or were they denying Christ? Kind of hard to decide so quickly isn't it? God looks upon the heart to determine if we are hot or cold.

He is merciful and we should not have fear of our human emotion nullifying our faith. God knows we are weak, fallible and at times even "chicken hearted". We prove out our faith in our daily walk with Jesus Christ. We can boldly go to the throne and ask God to deliver us from controlling fears that keep us from doing what we should, causing us to appear foolish and weak. I'm in no way condoning or advocating cowardice; I only want to highlight the mercy of God is greater than our fears. We should resist measuring ourselves by the actions of others and expect to something to happen because of it. We are not the standard to measure others actions by. Each of us has different strengths and abilities. We should seek to unify and encourage each other, comfort the fearful and feeble minded not accuse them. How many of us could honestly say we know how we would act if in a situation like Shadrach, Meshack and Abednego when threatened with death in the fiery furnace? Regardless of your answer you are not any less righteous than these, in fact they are your brothers. Fear not, it is our heart God sees and He can see the difference between fear and rejection.

Wasted Life

A wasted Life is
A life not well lived
Confused by anger's smoke screen
Unwilling to forgive
Errant thoughts in bloom
Nourished by blind beliefs
Value of a life unappreciated
Stolen away by the thief
A doubled-edged sword
Anger of the wounded cuts deep
Persuading us from loving another
So our heart might never be free
A wasted life is
Life's efforts misplaced
Cultivated by hatred
Unacquainted with grace

We Were Not Always

We were not always free
To seek after the life
Preordained for you and for me
So He tarried on for many days
Extending our blessings 365 ways

We were not always the ones victorious
But weary from losing so many battles
Because we had not faith in victory before us
So through his abundant and amazing grace
He led us all from a desolate place

We were not always among the strong
A product of many choices unwise
Often tempted to where we did not belong
So by the power of His Holy Spirit
He gave new life and strength to live it

We were not always faithful
Ungrateful we ignored our loving creator
To do those things deadly but playful
So He gave vision, knowledge and true sight
That we can be watchmen through the night

What Are They Doing

Have you ever thought that God requires more from you than he does from most other Christians? Or found it hard to slack up while every one around you appears to be on cruise? It's not all bad new saints. Just think, if much is given to whom much is required, then could it be possible that we have not tapped into all that God has given us top do what he asks of us?

My wife and I have these conversations every now and then with these exact sentiments. I suppose there are many churches across the country where 10 percent of the congregation does 90 percent of the labor. We dive in with energy and purpose and eventually we tire and need rest but find very a lack of reinforcement. So we ask God a question that really we know the answer to.

The voice of discouragement is loud in its attempt to hold us back from doing what we clearly understand is the will of God for us. The same negative voice of the flesh wrestles within us pitting us against our brothers and sisters in Christ. Not seeking a solution but instead divisions; us against them. Already tired it doe not take much to offended or frustrate. But God has called us to peace and he says his grace is sufficient to sustain us. It is for the cause of Christ that we must endure and suffer, seeking after God and petitioning him to open our eyes so we can see just how much he has to offer us to sustain us.

It's an untiring attack we face from our enemy seeking to wear us out and discourage our faith and commitment. Tear down the support beams that are currently holding up the church. Weaken their resolve and make them lukewarm, fearful, or otherwise impotent in their calling. So we questions what we are doing "Those requirements are not realistic are they?" "Don't be so inflexible your way is not the only right way", "Your friends won't understand you, you're going to push them away, ease up on that Christian stuff and live a little, God will understand, he loves you" Satan tells us as he test the waters to see how far we will let him creep back into our heart. The voice of Satan is always on duty trying to convince you and I that we are too religious and we don't understand the realdesires and problems in the world.

Of all Satan's tactics, fear is the most threatening. Fear can make a monster out of the meekest person. Fear will cause a person to abandon all common sense, even if the right choice seems obvious. Fear will make a wise man accept an answer from a fool. Fear can cause a person to see shame where there is no reason to feel so. Fear can cause you and I to be offended in the face of public opinion over how God has called us to live. This is why I believe Jesus said if I seek to keep my life, I would lose it. If I seek to lose my life I will save it. Fact is if I'm preoccupied with being liked, accepted, or understood it will be very difficult and nearly impossible to do all that God requires of me with all my heart. Isn't it interesting that God requires us to love him with all our heart and Satan seeks to get us to do exactly the opposite by being half hearted Christians. If we give up then we are no better than the other Christians who are the sitting on the sidelines watching work get done. Don't let Satan use fear to take our focus from accomplishing what God has called us, even if we cant' see others doing.

What Stole Your Joy

When we get beside ourselves we can really allow ourselves to believe we are unfortunate cant we? We feel we are so unlucky or not as blessed as so and so. But what I'm thinking of is how many people would like to get a present for a love one or a friend, but are unable to afford even the simplest item. I was thinking about when I wake up in warm house on a holiday day how many will wake up in shelters for whatever reason placed them there.

I have many wonderful memories of celebrations from my childhood, and all of them relate to togetherness and family. I can vaguely remember most of the toys or gifts I got over the years. What has been firmly implanted in my mind however are all of the family traditions, fun and "rituals" throughout the years. Christ was born to reconciled us to God and join us together as a family. Sadly, many of us miss that very important point. It is blessed to be hospitable, to be kind, to be giving. All that we have is because of the mercy and grace of God. We can bless even grumpy people just by being who we are children of the living God and not expecting anything back in return!

For the past 20 years my family and I have been nomads of sorts. Moving from place to place in the military. It would have been easy to fret or become depressed over all missed the family gatherings back home. Jesus has taught me how to be grateful for what I have, and to recognize the family he gave me. He has taught me to see my entire blessedness in where I am. The grass is always greener from across the street, because we don't live over there and we don't have to take care of the yard in the heat of the day.

I challenge you to see what God has done and stop dwelling on what we don't have and be thankful to God for what we do have. Each of us have come a long way and need to be grateful for how far we have come in our walk with Christ. The man with no legs would love to have a limp. The woman desperately seeking a job would love to be tired because of a long day at work. Ask yourself this question. Do you have joy in your heart and life? If not, what stole your joy.

When The Grass Seems Greener

When was the last time you held a pity party and you were the only one invited? Sounds familiar? A great time for a pity party I've discovered is moving season, when friends and family are left behind as military families uproot and move on to new places and new challenges. Some families adjust quite well as I was blessed to be able to do for over two decades. But some of my friends and neighbors did not fare so well however, and I heard over and over their complaints and lament of "our last assignment was better" I usually ask them did they complain about their last assignment when they lived there and eventually they have to confess that they did.

They are suffering from what I have come to term "the last assignment was better syndrome." Or the grass is greener on the other side of the street. The symptoms are obvious and can be easily detected. Most notably it's when there is constant complaint about ones present job and home and how bad it is compared to a former job and home. We become so focused on the negatives that we couldn't see any positives if they were pained on our forehead while we were facing a mirror.

The grass always looks greener across the street until you cross over and see all the weeds growing in your neighbor's yard. The vacation brochures always look better than the actual location when you arrive. Life is like that and other people will always seem to have it all together. And do you know what, to some people you and I are the other people with all the green grass.

We make a determination that the lives of others are perfect while looking from the outside. It's not their fault that we want to be in their shoes without knowing what the fit will be like. It is quite foolish to lace up the shoes of another without knowledge of where they have walked and where they still must walk. In the vanity and futility of our minds we just like the way it looks on them. Anyone who has done any type of lawn care will tell you there is a lot of hard work and sweat with far too little time available to do it. Keeping a lawn green and healthy takes much care and much watching and waiting. When a lawn is truly green and weed free it did not happen overnight.

Truthfully some lawns look healthy when they are not just as some people look healthy when they are not. We cannot live our life based on what we think we see. We cannot make choices base on what we observe. Life teaches us that some things are not as they seem. Yet every day friends and loved ones vainly imagine themselves to be in a worse situation than every other person in the neighborhood or every other member in the church. Everyone's grass is greener and they spend so much time looking at it that they neglect their own.

A testimony or shared conversation from that neighbor across the street often dispels the myths in our minds. We find that they have problems too with the brown spots in their lawn, which interestingly can at times look very similar to those in our yard. We need balance and it helps to count our blessing and remember those who are worse off than we are as much as we imagine those who are better off.

When we get the urge to complain about our jobs and our homes, remember to thank God for being employed otherwise there would not be a job to complain about. Focus on that which is praise worthy, the true things, the honest things, the pure and lovely things. Think about the good things in your life. If we want green grass in our lives then focus on what God has done and is doing for us and be thankful. Spend a little time in our own yard. Water our own garden with words of encouragement. Fertilize the flowers of our life; family and friends that bring a sweet aroma to your existence. Kill off the weeds of envy, dissension, pity and ungratefulness with the word of God planted firmly in you. Trim the lawn and hedges with kindness and hospitality toward others. Next time we are looking around we may find our focus is admirably fixed to our yard and our life with a big smile.

Who Am I

Childhood memories play like special features
In a DVD they come as highlights and flashes
Attempting to tell the whole story
Without going into detail, like promo movies
What you see isn't necessarily a true image
What happened who am I really I seek truth
My father was my father, then he wasn't
Then he was again, I've come full circle
To find the truth of my identity
Lies have deceived and confused me
My heart still harbors no hate or animosity
I'm still seeking the truth to dispel my curiosity
Determined, I drive purposely toward answers
I arrive at an intersection called mom and dad

Who Do You Say I Am

Over the years faces known and unknown gathered with me in one place together
Wearing coordinated fashions that were on occasion mistaken for sincere passion
Though I showed my face once or twice, I was never really there
I heard the story evolve but my heart always remained unmoved by his crown
of thorns
Was I blind to his sufferings, in ignorance I sat unaware, of every stripe that he bear
Lashes that were destined to my debt, had he not given me chance to be reborn
Without a mumbling word I'm told, that he stood in willingly in my stead
Yet absurdly I behaved as though I had not heard, of him the living word
Like many around me the savior was a stranger, and to us all but dead
Would this April foolishness remain a part of my reality?
True meaning negated and evaporated each year out of my consciousness
Woe is me Lord, Woe is me, a man undone, truth I'm unable to see
Can anyone show me, tell me of his resurrection power
What will it mean, when I am rescued from this heartless routine?
Surely true worship of the savior demands more than a few hours
God did reveal to my heart his wonderful love and magnificent glory
Truth lives on still, one's heart can know who Jesus is
His death and resurrection gives me freedom to tell the whole story
Will others be reminded of Jesus, am I an adequate witness for Christ
Will my message speak of eggs and rabbits, or well-established habits?
No, my message must be of his death and resurrection, the true source of life

Who's On First

Who's on first
Is it you, is it me
Is it us, is it He
Men and women battle
Wrestling life's situations
grappling for control
So Who's on first
Is the reflection of expectations
Our motivation for the current situation
Men nor women, neither submits
strong-willed adversaries
Confidently walking the road to destruction
The two who were made to be one
lay fragmented, none able to stand
Prostrated and powerless
Who's on first, tell me again
What only God can do
Resist the urge to entrust to man

Xmas Lie

It was the night before Xmas
Because no one wanted to offend
People were generous giving a little extra
But none dared mention the Son of Man
Fewer acknowledge the true reason
None humble enough to kneel down
To give praise to the creator
Believing that prayer had no place in their town
Mesmerized by secular celebrations
Some thought little of Christ's birth
All year they'd waited in anticipation
For the biggest holiday celebration on earth
They ignored the significance of the event
Instead they focused on buying gifts
Dreading how much money they'd spent
Rejoicing in whom they spend the holiday with
Around town people could be heard singing
About peace on earth and holiday greetings
There were rare references to the Lord Jesus
Substituted with politically corrected meanings
But the festivities, diamonds and gold
Could never be enough to justify
The misery awaiting every deceived soul
Who rejects the truth for the Xmas lie

About the Author

His interest in writing can be traced back to high school creative writing class in Wilmington North Carolina. And for as long as he can remember he has used writing as a way of expressing his thoughts. In 1993 while stationed in Germany he started an email devotional with the purpose of encouraging friends who were far from home serving their country and fighting battles of depression and stress on occasion. Remembering that a Pastor once noted him before the congregation stating that he was an inspiration, and would call him Barnabas after the biblical character in the bible who's life was spent encouraging others. Those few kind words have always stuck with him, and encouraged him in his writing.